Johnson's Life Of Milton: With Introduction And Notes

Samuel Johnson

JOHNSON'S
LIFE OF MILTON

WITH INTRODUCTION AND NOTES

BY

F. RYLAND, M.A.

AUTHOR OF "A STUDENT'S HANDBOOK OF PSYCHOLOGY AND ETHICS,"
"CHRONOLOGICAL OUTLINES OF ENGLISH
LITERATURE," ETC.

LONDON
GEORGE BELL & SONS
1894

PREFACE.

IN the Notes to these editions of Johnson's "Lives" the Editor has endeavoured to consider not only the wants of young students, but also those of older readers, who may wish to know the authorities on which Johnson's statements are based. For the first time, nearly all the author's facts, and nearly all his quotations, have been traced back to their original sources, and chapter and verse given for them. The annotations of Cunningham and later editors have been very largely supplemented; and the present Editor ventures to believe that his work will be of service to all readers of the "Lives."

PUTNEY.

INTRODUCTION.

I. LIFE OF JOHNSON.

SAMUEL JOHNSON was born at Lichfield on September 18th, 1709. His father, Michael Johnson, was a bookseller, who, at one time a well-to-do magistrate of the city, fell before his death into distressed circumstances. He was a high churchman and a Tory, with Jacobite leanings.

The child's physical organization was undermined by scrofula, the king's evil as it was then called, which afterwards scarred and distorted his features and left him a prey to extreme mental depression and other symptoms of nervous disease. As he grew older he was afflicted with convulsive movements, and he lost the sight of one eye. About his fifth year—he could not have been six—he was brought to London to be touched for the evil by Queen Anne. He was sent to Lichfield Grammar School, then under a very severe master, Mr. Hunter, one of the Cathedral clergy. He afterwards went to Stourbridge Grammar School (in Worcestershire), where he remained a year; but his school days were over at the age of sixteen. A couple of years at home were spent in desultory reading, " not voyages and travels" (he told Boswell), " but all literature, Sir, all ancient writers, all manly; though but little Greek . . . . so that when I came to Oxford, Dr. Adams, now Master of

Pembroke College, told me I was the best qualified for the
University that he had ever known come there." [1]

He went up to Oxford (Pembroke College), in the
October of 1728, and he remained there, according to
Boswell, until the autumn of 1731, although Croker and
other recent authorities [2] believe that he left the University
after only fourteen months' residence, in December, 1729.
Who supplied the necessary funds for his University course
is still an unsolved question; it could hardly have been his
father, who was very badly off, and who died in an
insolvent condition in 1731. However long he remained
at the University, Johnson took no degree. He seems to
have been a somewhat troublesome undergraduate; as a
rough and self-reliant lad with the learning of a don might
easily become. But he fell under the influence of that
half-forgotten High Church revival which preceded the
great Evangelical movement of the Wesleys; and religion
became a great reality for him after he had read William
Law's " Serious Call to a Holy Life."

After his departure from Oxford and the death of his
father, Johnson passed a year of struggle, apparently without definite occupation except during the few months he
spent as usher in the Grammar School of Market Bosworth,
months of " complicated misery " which he recalled with
" even a degree of horror." [3] In 1733 he went to stay for
six months with his old school-fellow Hector, now a surgeon
at Birmingham. Here he was thrown into the company of
the chief bookseller of the town; and this circumstance
seems to have led him to take up literary work. He
settled in Birmingham, and in the next year or two wrote
contributions for a sort of local " Spectator," besides translating and abridging Father Lobo's " Voyage to Abyssinia "
from a French translation. In 1735 he married Mrs. Porter,

---

[1] Boswell, Bohn, i. 30.   [2] Boswell, Bohn, i. 405-409.
                    [3] Boswell, Bohn, i. 50.

the widow of a Birmingham tradesman. The bride was forty-eight, the bridegroom not quite twenty-six. But Johnson declared long afterwards [1] that it "was a love marriage on both sides," and the married life of the strangely assorted pair seems to have been very happy. "Tetty" had a fortune of about £800, and on this pecuniary basis Johnson set up a school at Edial, near Lichfield. He had only a few pupils (Boswell says three) one of whom was David Garrick. The school was soon seen to be a failure, and in the spring of 1737 Johnson and Garrick came to London to seek their fortunes.

Johnson brought with him part of a tragedy, "Irene," which it was his first business to finish. But the play did not see the light till 1749.

Several years' experience as a hack-writer, a doer of literary odd jobs, lay before Johnson. At that date journalism was not a lucrative profession, if, indeed, such a profession can be said to have existed at all. Although Johnson soon got work on Cave's "Gentleman's Magazine," one of the best of the monthly periodicals, he must have had a hard and anxious time for a year or so. However, Boswell thinks that in 1738 he was already earning "a tolerable livelihood." [2] In 1738 his wife joined him in London, and in 1738 too came honour as well as guineas. On the same morning as Pope's "Epilogue to the Satires" appeared Johnson's "London," an imitation of Juvenal's third satire. The work of the new writer was not eclipsed by that of the most illustrious literary man of the age, and in a week a new edition of Johnson's poem was called for. A life of Father Paul Sarpi, the historian of the Council of Trent, was his first important contribution to the "Gentleman's Magazine," and afterwards (1739-43) he wrote for it short biographies of Drake, Blake,

---

[1] Boswell, Bohn, i. 60.   [2] Boswell, Bohn, i. 78.

Sydenham, and others, literary criticism and miscellaneous essays, and reported the debates in Parliament, or rather worked them up from such rough notes as could be furnished by persons paid to attend. In 1744 he produced a life of Richard Savage, a Bohemian literary man who had been his friend, and who had died the year before. This biography was afterwards embodied in the "Lives of the Poets."

In 1747 Johnson issued his "Plan for a Dictionary of the English Language," addressed to Philip Dormer, Earl of Chesterfield. The great dictionary, which was published by a group of booksellers, what would now-a-days be called a syndicate of publishers, occupied most of his time for the next seven years. He got little or no help from Chesterfield, and as he had to employ six clerks the expenses were considerable. Most of the 1,500 guineas which the booksellers had contracted to pay him were received on account before the work appeared.

"The Vanity of Human Wishes," an imitation of Juvenal's tenth satire, appeared in the January of 1749, and in February "Irene" was at length produced on the stage of Drury Lane by Garrick, who had deserted the law, for which he was intended, and had become the greatest actor and theatrical manager of the day. The tragedy was not a success, but thanks to the kindly zeal of Garrick, it ran for nine nights, and Johnson's share of the receipts, together with the payment for press rights, amounted to very nearly £300. From March, 1750, to March, 1752, he issued twice a week a periodical essay called the "Rambler;" there existed many such imitations *longo intervallo* of the "Spectator," some grave and some gay, and Johnson's was the most serious of all. His wife, much loved and long lamented, died on the day on which the last "Rambler" appeared. Although not very popular during its serial publication, it proved a great success when collected in volumes, and on it was founded Johnson's reputation as a moralist.

In 1755 the Dictionary at last saw the light, in two great folio volumes. Since that day, philology has become scientific, and the crude etymologies of Johnson provoke the mirth of modern scholars. But his Dictionary is an enormous advance on its incomplete and unsatisfactory predecessors. Just before it appeared, when he began "to see land after having wandered in this vast sea of words,"[1] the University of Oxford granted him an M.A. degree, and he was now recognized as at the head of the literary world of London. He continued to write for the magazines, and to one of them, the weekly "Universal Chronicle," contributed during 1758-1760 the series of essays known as the "Idler." His gloomy oriental story "Rasselas" was written "in the evenings of a single week," in the early spring of 1759, in order "to defray the expense of his mother's funeral and pay some little debts which she had left."[2] Besides these and miscellaneous reviews and essays, he wrote prefaces to books, dedications, addresses, and speeches.

In 1762 he received a pension of £300 a year from the crown in recognition of his literary labours; and now at last at the age of fifty-three he was put beyond the need of daily toil for his daily bread. Henceforth he wrote comparatively little.

Although he wrote little, he talked much; and he became the centre of a brilliant group of eminent men who honoured him and loved his society. The famous Literary Club was founded by Sir Joshua Reynolds and Johnson in 1764, and originally consisted of twelve members, among whom were Burke, Goldsmith, Topham Beauclerk (a dissipated man of fashion), Bennet Langton (a gentleman and a

---

[1] Boswell, Bohn, i. 216.　　　[2] Boswell, Bohn, i. 269.

scholar with "a mind as exalted as his stature"), and Sir John Hawkins, the author of a "History of Music." The numbers were afterwards increased several times; but in 1780 the maximum was fixed at forty. Boswell, Garrick, Gibbon, Sheridan, Percy, Adam Smith, Sir William Scott (Lord Stowell), Sir William Jones, and the Wartons, were amongst the early members. Until 1783 the club met at the "Turk's Head" in Gerrard Street, Soho.

Johnson's conversation has been preserved for us by the zeal and industry of James Boswell, a young Scotch advocate, whose "Life of Dr. Johnson" is not only the best biography, but perhaps in the words of Macaulay "the most delightful narrative in the language." Boswell was a bright, intelligent and amiable young man with a passion for pushing his acquaintance among interesting people. He was somewhat vain, and unaffectedly undignified, and there was about him a want of reserve which amounted to a kind of intellectual immodesty. But his weaknesses endear him to his readers, and his book is great just because he had the important qualifications of unsparing diligence and acute perception, real insight into character, true admiration for greatness, and the gift of easy and pleasant narration. Meeting Johnson in the May of 1763, he has left us a wonderful record of the last twenty-one years of the great man's life.

Johnson was a conversational gladiator; he talked, as he owned, for victory. He loved a paradox in conversation though he disliked it in print, because it made an immediate impression, and gave an instant opportunity for a battle of words. This made him glory in his prejudices and exaggerate them. In his view of life he was, to some extent, what we now call a pessimist; he suffered much from ill-health and depression. But he had "a noble and a true conceit of god-like amity." Surrounded by his friends, he appears like a Christian Socrates, a wise and tolerant old man, mingling freely in the everyday enjoyment of his younger companions, without any dyspeptic protests against such of their pleasures as he thought fit not to share.

In 1765 he came to know Mr. Thrale, the proprietor of a great brewery, a rich man and a member of parliament. Much of Johnson's time during the next sixteen or seventeen years was spent at Mr. Thrale's house at Streatham. His wife, Hester Lynch Thrale, a charming little lady, full of high spirits, did much to make Johnson happy, and "his irregular habits" as Boswell says, were "lessened by association with an agreeable and well ordered family." [1] The University of Dublin gave him the degree of LL.D. in the year 1765, and ten years afterwards his own University gave him a doctor's degree in laws. His edition of "Shakespeare" was published in 1765 with an important preface. In 1770 he produced a political pamphlet with reference to the expulsion of Wilkes from the House of Commons, the "False Alarm;" this was next year followed by another, "Thoughts on the Late Transactions respecting Falkland's Islands." A third, "Taxation no Tyranny," 1775, maintained the right of the British parliament to tax the American colonists. None of these produced any effect, however momentary.

At the age of sixty-four (1773), Johnson took with Boswell a long tour in the Highlands of Scotland and the Hebrides. This was quite an adventurous expedition for an unwieldy man of his years, at a time when roads and wheeled carriages were unknown in the islands; and the "Great Cham of Literature" underwent not only a great deal of discomfort, but some considerable danger. But he went through it all with patience and good humour; and he has left us an account of it in his "Journey to the Western Islands of Scotland" (1775), although most people

[1] Boswell, Bohn, ii. 17.

will prefer to read Boswell's gossiping and lively "Journal of a Tour to the Hebrides." In 1774 Dr. Johnson went with the Thrales on a tour in Wales, and in 1775 he visited France with them.

His last literary undertaking was to write Prefaces, biographical and critical, to the works of the English poets, included by the syndicate of booksellers in their great edition of 1779-1781. These Prefaces were soon republished as "Lives of the English Poets." Johnson was not responsible for the selection of names, though it was at his suggestion that the works of Blackmore, Watts, Pomfret, and Yalden were added; a selection which excludes the great Elizabethans and the amatory and religious poets of the mid seventeenth century. Chaucer, and Spenser, and Shakespeare, Herrick, and Herbert are indeed absent; but then have we not Walsh and "Rag" Smith, Duke and King, and Sprat? The work was done very unevenly, and is very unequal in value. There was not very much consultation of unpublished authorities. But he used Spence's MS. Collection of Anecdotes, lent by the Duke of Newcastle; and he was at some little pains to insert gossip and personal reminiscences, which would otherwise have vanished. The "Lives" remain our chief authority for many of the minor writers; while no modern biographer can afford to neglect the accounts given by Johnson of the great writers of the early eighteenth century. Of the criticism contained in the book, something will be said presently.

During the half-century he spent in London, Johnson had lived in nearly a score of different places. At first he changed his lodgings frequently. After his wife joined him in 1738 he lived in Castle Street, which runs parallel with Oxford Street; and then in the Strand and in several of the adjoining streets, in Holborn, in Gough Square (1748-1758), in Staple Inn, in Gray's Inn, then for five

years in Inner Temple Lane (1760-1765), in Johnson's
Court, Fleet Street (1765-1777), and in Bolt Court, Fleet
Street, for the last seven years of his life. In his house
he had accumulated an extraordinary group of feeble and
unfortunate people, whom he treated with great kindness
and charity: Robert Levett, a broken-down medical man,
in whose skill Johnson professed the greatest trust; Miss
Williams, a pale, shrunken old lady afflicted with blindness; Mrs. Desmoulins and her daughter, to whom he
allowed half-a-guinea a week, and Miss Carmichael. These
inmates gave Johnson unnecessary trouble by their frequent
quarrels. He told Mrs. Thrale on one occasion: "Williams
hates everybody; Levett hates Desmoulins and does not
love Williams: Desmoulins hates them both; Poll loves
none of them." [1]

In 1781 he lost his friend Mr. Thrale, who had made
Johnson one of his executors. Mrs. Thrale soon formed an
attachment to an Italian musician named Piozzi, and in
the interests of her children as well as herself Johnson
opposed this union. In 1784, however, she married, much
against Johnson's wish, and their friendship was at an
end. He suffered a great deal from asthma and sleepless-
ness. After visiting Oxford, Lichfield, and Birmingham
in the summer, he was taken worse in November, and died
on December 13th, 1784, aged 75.

Johnson was one of the most honest and independent of
men; his powerful, masculine nature, and his hatred of
unreality sometimes led him to speak with almost brutal
violence; but there was a great depth of tenderness under
his rough exterior. People of narrow natures perceived
only the outside. Mrs. Boswell said to her husband: "I
have seen many a bear led by a man, but I never before
saw a man led by a bear." [2] But Goldsmith had keener

[1] Boswell, Bohn, iii. 363.   [2] Boswell, Bohn, ii. 249.

insight when he said, "He has nothing of the bear but the skin."[1] He had the firmest convictions in religion and politics; he disliked Whiggism and dissent; but some of his greatest friends were Whigs, and some of his favourite authors were Nonconformists. We need not (with Macaulay) call him a bigot, because he practised abstinence on Good Friday. Judged by the standard of the age his mind was singularly free from superstitions, political and theological. He was less superstitious than Doddridge or Wesley, and other pious contemporaries, and who shall complain of his conditional belief in the Cock Lane ghost, a belief necessarily assumed merely for the purpose of examination, in these days of the Psychical Society?

"One thing he did," says Leigh Hunt, "perhaps beyond any man in England before or since—he advanced, by the powers of his conversation, the strictness of his veracity, and the respect he exacted towards his presence, what may be called the personal dignity of literature."

II. JOHNSON'S CRITICISM.

Johnson's literary attitude is that of the average practical man, caught young and educated. He accepts the critical standards of the age, without much misgiving, and seldom goes behind them to ask the why and the wherefore. In the words of Macaulay he "decided literary questions like a lawyer, not like a legislator." Now-a-days the critics try to decide them like philosophers, or men of science.

The main object of modern criticism is to show us how to understand, and how to enjoy, literary or artistic work. It strives to trace the special laws which underlie the

---

[1] Boswell, Bohn, ii. 76.

different kinds of excellence. It does not assume that
great literary achievement is always dependent on the same
conditions, that there are any universal and necessary
canons of beauty which will be always exemplified in the
finest work. The best modern critics approach a great poem
somewhat as men of science approach a fact of nature.
The duty of the critic is to analyze the complex effect
produced on us, and to exhibit separately the conditions of
its production. Although we may recognize that some
types of beauty are more impressive, or more insistent, or
more complete, than others, it is not for the critic to classify
literary works as good or bad merely because they embody
the particular ideals which he regards as most perfect.[1]
Many critics do not accept this view of their functions
even now. In the eighteenth century scarcely any accepted
it. They pronounced a judgment on a work because it
was, or was not, in accordance with the literary ideals then
accepted. They did not stop to inquire whether there
were other literary ideals equally valid.

The literary models of the eighteenth century were determined by three principal factors—regard for morality,
regard for the classics, and regard for the opinion of
the average plain man; in other words, by edification,
correctness, and common sense. And the greatest of these
three was common sense.

On the first of the ideals there is no need to say much.
When we find Dennis laying down that it is the " duty of
every tragic poet . . . . to inculcate a particular Providence," we see that he carries the union of Church and
Stage to a very exacting degree. When Dr. Johnson
grumbles at Gray's " Bard," because it does not "promote
any truth, moral or political," we are struck with the

[1] On what has been called Inductive Criticism, see Professor
R. G. Moulton's "Shakespeare as a Dramatic Artist," Introduction.

cramping effect on literature of this insatiable desire
for edification. We are reminded of the senior wrangler
who had been induced to read "Paradise Lost," and who
returned the book with the remark that he did not see what
it proved. The eighteenth century did not believe in art
for art's sake. It was still dominated by Puritan scruples.
Defoe lards his "Moll Flanders" with pious reflections—
often half ironical, as it seems to the modern reader ; while
"Pamela" is "published in order to cultivate the principles
of Virtue and Religion in the Minds of the Youth of Both
Sexes," and Swift himself, the supreme master of cynical
humour, defends the "Beggar's Opera" in all seriousness
as "an excellent moral performance."

The term "correctness," so often used by the eighteenth
century critics, is difficult to explain. It involves perfec-
tion of technique, the avoidance of all inadequacies and
excesses of form ; the achievement of clearness and pre-
cision in language, metre, and rhyme, and in what may be
called the anatomy of epic and tragedy. There must be
the proper word in the proper place ; the right number of
syllables in the line ; the rhymes must be true ; the work
must begin and end in the proper way ; the story must be
told within the proper limitations as to length, number of
books or acts, number of characters, and so forth. The
ideal aimed at, the approximation to which constituted correctness, was, however, not quite clearly defined. It was
partly due to study of the French poets and critics of the
reign of Louis XIV., and partly to the study of the sources
from which these derived their inspiration, the classical
poets and critics.

A dread of all strong feeling and of any vividness of expression which was likely to be regarded as hyperbolical in
a very conventional age, went along with a dislike of the
unsophisticated, the merely ordinary and simple. On the
one hand there was the Scylla of "enthusiasm," on the other

the Charybdis of the "familiar" and the "gross." Hence the absence of any fanciful or passionate lyrical poetry, hence the frigid decorum of the epics and tragedies. A special poetical diction followed as a matter of course; the poet required a "system of words at once refined from the grossness of domestic use, and free from the harshness of terms appropriated to particular arts."[1]

Lord Macaulay in his boisterous attack on "correctness" in the essay on Moore's "Life of Byron,"[2] makes two mistakes. He regards poetry as a purely imitative art; and he assumes that a purely imitative art is freed from all allegiance to the ideal. Now poetry is at once a representative art like sculpture or painting, and a presentative art like music. Its object is not merely to put before us scenes which are not present and events which we have never witnessed, but to create for the ear beautiful melodies and harmonies of verse. It affects our emotions not only by what it puts before the visual imagination, but also by its appeal to the auditory and muscular sensations of tone and rhythm. Macaulay's second error is more important. An imitative or representative art is not absolved from all regard for beauty; its sole aim is not accuracy of reproduction. Even a photograph is largely idealistic: prose, background and accessories, lighting, degree of detail, these points, and many more, require consideration and selection; and selection implies an ideal. The object of the photographer, and à fortiori of the painter or the poet, is not to produce an exact representation, but to produce a representation sufficiently exact to form the starting point of waves of suggestion. And the direction of these waves he controls by the exclusion of what is commonplace, or exaggerated, or unpleasant. And in this need for avoiding what clashes with our sense of

[1] Johnson's "Lives," Bohn, i. 435.
[2] "Essays," pp. 148-151.

beauty, we have the justification of rules, or rather principles, of "correct" form.

But these rules, like the principles of morality, tend to
be regarded as good in and for themselves. The critics
come to think that merit lies in the obedience to rule, and
not in the achievement of what the rule was intended to
secure. Comply with all the precepts laid down by Aristotle
and Longinus, by Horace and Boileau, and your work will
be perfect and immortal.

Much, indeed, of the eighteenth century poetry is simply
unreadable; not, however, because it conforms to arbitrary
rules, but because the poetical impulse which produced it
was weak and chill. When a man of poetical genius like
Pope, or Gray, or Goldsmith, writes, his work gains at
least as much as it loses by compliance with fixed canons
of literary form. What it surrenders in energy of expression and uncalculated felicity of achievement is made up to
it by dignity, suggestiveness, and restraint. We have long
since seen the end of that reaction against literary form
which is exemplified by what Mr. Jacobs[1] terms the
"amorphous masses called poems" produced by Southey
and, we may add, Wordsworth. Many of our poets to-day
are as much formalists as any of the eighteenth century
writers; Tennyson, Matthew Arnold, Austin Dobson, each
is, after his own kind, a supreme master of technique.

But, notwithstanding the reverence for correctness,
common sense is the central ideal in eighteenth century literature and criticism. It is the final test of excellence. "By the common sense of readers uncorrupted
with literary prejudices, after all the refinement of subtlety and the dogmatism of learning, must be finally
decided all claim to poetical honours."[2] The Augustan
age was eminently a social one. The tastes of the best

[1] "Tennyson and 'In Memoriam,'" by Joseph Jacobs, p. 6.
[2] Johnson's "Lives," Bohn, iii. 384.

and most conventional classes in a well-organized State formed the standard which Addison, and Pope, and Richardson had before them. Corsairs and outlaws and peasants were to be the ideal figures of the reaction under Byron and Scott and Wordsworth, after Rousseau had taught that the "state of nature" was superior to the social condition. To the men of the eighteenth century the "state of nature" presented few attractions. Their worship of common sense was due to their respect for properly ordered society. The beliefs of the vast majority of such a society tend to become alike, one type of opinion is formed. *My* common sense is the reflection in me of the average opinions of other plain men. "Quod semper, quod ubique, quod ab omnibus" becomes the criterion of truth. It requires a man of extraordinary courage to question beliefs so universal. They are found to fit in with the needs of practical life, and Berkeley is refuted with a kick. Science is freed from the "jargon" of technical terms; and philosophy is to be "brought out of closets and libraries, schools and colleges, to dwell in clubs and assemblies, at tea-tables, and coffee-houses." Superficiality incarnate in the person of Tillotson occupies the pulpit.

It is, however, common sense which saves Johnson from being a pedant. Correctness is no doubt important, but common sense is still more important. He is quite prepared to criticise Aristotle, if Aristotle is in conflict with common sense. He does not, like Dryden or even Addison, quote Bossu and Boileau with bated breath.

Johnson's criticism is thus usually right when he lays down some general truth of form, or deals with some question of formal consistency. He can point out contradictions, errors of reasoning, and errors of fact, faulty similes and imperfect rhymes. He falls short only when imagination and sympathy are required. He has not that fine natural insight into unfamiliar modes of action and feeling which

makes a critic of the highest order. That alert perception
of beauty which comes from ready sympathy with the
artistic aims of others is absent; he sees only that a rule
is broken, that a formal absurdity has been perpetrated;
the beauty which it strives to embody escapes him.
Speaking generally, we may say that what he lays down in
criticism is true as far as it goes. It is not the whole
truth, of course; no man ever sees the whole truth, and
certainly no one proposition can ever contain the whole
truth. But it is a part of the truth which it is unsafe to
neglect.

What he says, for instance, about poetical diction [1] is
true enough: "Words too familiar or too remote defeat
the purpose of a poet. From those sounds which we hear
on small or on coarse occasions we do not easily receive
strong impressions or delightful images; and words to
which we are nearly strangers, whenever they occur, draw
that attention on themselves which they should transmit
to things." But when he comes from laying down
these general laws to apply them to particular cases he
is liable to overlook the special circumstances. His condemnation of Dryden's nautical phraseology is undoubtedly too unqualified; he has not appreciated the
superior vividness which results from the use of such highly
specialized language. His condemnation of the over-
elaborated and frigid conceits of the metaphysical school
is as good as possible,[2] but their fine lyrical talent he
seems scarcely to have noticed, much less to have
felt. He calls attention to Gray's occasional failure in a
forced metaphor or simile and to what he happily calls the
"eumbrous splendour" of the odes, but he has no ear for
Gray's bright picturesqueness of phrase and his fine subtlety
of rhythm.

[1] "Lives," Bohn, i. 435 (compare i. 448).
[2] "Lives," Bohn, i. 24, 52.

Johnson again is entirely right to point out that the pastoral form and the allegorical allusions of "Lycidas" are highly artificial, and give a tone of unreality to the poem. "Passion plucks no berries from the myrtle and ivy, nor calls upon Arethusa and Mincius. Where there is leisure for fiction there is little grief. . . . Its form is that of a pastoral . . . . whatever images it can supply are long ago exhausted, and its inherent improbability always forces dissatisfaction on the mind." Yet, we ask, by what fatality does the critic come to utter in reference to "Lycidas" those truths which, if applied to the pastorals of Pope or Philips, we should not attempt to resist? And what are we to think of Johnson's capacity for directly perceiving beauty, when he adds, " surely no man could have fancied that he read 'Lycidas' with pleasure had he not known the author." [1] This surely is letting his judgment get the better of him with a vengeance.

But after we have made all the necessary deductions, Johnson's criticism remains full of value, and especially for us. In periods when imagination and emotion are dominant in literature, and when men take most delight in just those literary elements which are least allied to pure reason, it is necessary that we should be sometimes recalled to the recognition of its more orderly, abstract and intellectual elements. Though the formal aspects of literature have not all the importance which the eighteenth century assigned to them, they have much more importance than the nineteenth is inclined to attribute to them. And nothing is more likely to enforce this on us than the grave sanity, the practical knowledge of the world, and the moral elevation of Johnson's criticism.

[1] "Lives," Bohn, i. 167, 168.

III. JOHNSON'S STYLE.

It is usually said that Johnson's style is highly latinized, and that it delights in polysyllables. This is certainly not true of the "Lives of the Poets;" though it has some slight foundation as applied to the "Rambler."

The following results were obtained from examining four passages (each of 200 lines) in each of the works mentioned:—

In the " Rambler: "
    30·5 per cent. of words of classical origin.
    19   „   „   of more than two syllables.
In the " Lives of the Poets: "
    28·7 per cent. of words of classical origin.
    13·1 „   „   of more than two syllables.
In Macaulay's " Essays: "
    28·6 per cent. of words of classical origin.
    16·5 „   „   of more than two syllables.
In two critical articles in the " Athenæum " (1893):
    28·5 per cent. of words of classical origin.
    17·5 „   „   of more than two syllables.

It will be noticed that the proportion of words of classical and Romance origin in the " Lives " is almost exactly the same as the proportion of these words in Macaulay, and in the reviewers of to-day. In the use of long words Johnson is actually more sparing than Macaulay and the writer in the " Athenæum." He has, I fancy, got his reputation for excessive Latinism from his habit of employing these long words just where most writers would use short ones; his familiar passages are much fuller of four-syllable words than those of the other writers mentioned, but he reduces his average by indulging in fewer polysyllables than the more modern writers, when he comes to a more formal and technical passage. It is probably this employment of long and sonorous classical words when we expect short and unobtrusive English ones, which helps to give the impression of stiffness and ponderosity.

Thus for "greediness" he says "avidity," and for "freeing" he says "manumission;" "cool courage" he renders by "deliberate intrepidity," and instead of calling a translation "too free," he terms it "licentiously paraphrastical."

Allied with this is his tendency to use the abstract for the concrete, e.g., "Whiggism" for "Whigs." He tells us that Milton's "natural port is gigantic loftiness," or that Warburton "excelled in critical perspicacity," where adverbs and adjectives would do at least as well. And he is fond of writing a couple of abstract nouns where most writers would employ only one linked with an adjective: e.g., he speaks of "imprudence of generosity or vanity of profusion" instead of "imprudent generosity or vain profusion." Similar to these are such sentences as follow:—"No writer had yet undertaken to reform either the savageness of neglect or the impertinence of civility;" "He never spared any asperity of reproach or brutality of insolence." And he speaks of an attempt "to represent the whole course of things as a necessary concatenation of indissoluble fatality."

Johnson's sentences are seldom long. There are none of the cumbrous and involved clauses, in which our writers from Hooker to Locke, so frequently delighted. If a sentence exceed three lines, it is usually broken up by semicolons into co-ordinate and virtually unconnected parts.

But these uninvolved sentences are not always natural in

structure. Johnson is fond of inversion; and a favourite
device of his is that of beginning a sentence with a pre-
positional phrase: "To a thousand cavils one answer is
sufficient." "Of the first stanza the abrupt beginning has
been celebrated." Or he begins with a dependent clause:
"When the Hanoverian succession was disputed, Tickell
gave what assistance his pen would supply." "That in the
reigns of Charles and James the 'Paradise Lost' received
no public acclamations is readily confessed." He gives an
appearance of inversion to some sentences by omitting the
impersonal "it" we usually employ when the real subject
is a noun clause. Instead of saying "It is to be lamented
that——" he writes, "That this poem was never written is
reasonably to be lamented."

The late Professor Minto[1] points out that Johnson is
fond of "abruptly introducing a general principle before
the particular circumstance that it applies to." This
peculiarity, he adds, was adopted by Macaulay, whose
style owes more to that of Johnson than is usually
acknowledged. In fact, we may say that Macaulay's style
is Johnson's, broken into short spasmodic sentences, freed
from inversion, and rendered concrete.

Antithesis and balance are constantly employed. Opposed terms are set over against each other; and a strict
parallelism is observed in order to emphasize the opposition. No English writer since the time of Lyly had employed this rhetorical artifice to the same extent. No writer
until Macaulay employed it again to the same extent. After
the lumbering and trailing clauses of the seventeenth century, it is delightful to get these clear-cut epigrams: "He
thought woman made only for obedience, and man only
for rebellion." "He hated monarchs in the State, and
prelates in the Church; for he hated all whom he was

---

[1] "English Prose Writers." (Johnson.)

required to obey." "He was never reduced to the necessity of soliciting the sun to shine upon a birthday, of
calling the graces to a wedding, or of saying what multitudes had said before him. When he could produce
nothing new, he was at liberty to be silent." "Pope
was not content to satisfy; he dared to excel, and therefore always endeavoured to do his best; he did not
court the candour, but dared the judgment of his reader;
and expecting no indulgence from others, he showed none
to himself." It is easy to multiply such passages; and,
indeed, it must be owned that much of their effect is lost
by the frequency with which they are repeated.[1]

Among the occasional faults of Johnson's style we may
note his careless employment of the pronouns of the third
person, a laxity common enough with the writers of the
eighteenth century. One instance will suffice. Speaking
of Pope and Warburton, Dr. Johnson tells us that:—"He
[Pope] introduced him [Warburton] to Mr. Murray, by
whose interest he became preacher at Lincoln's Inn, and
to Mr. Allen, who gave him his niece and his estate, and
by consequence a bishopric. When he died he left him
the property of his works." The confusion and ambiguity
could scarcely be worse. Another fault which sometimes
occurs, is one of sentence structure. Although Johnson's
sentences are usually short, they sometimes take the form
of a long and loosely connected string of statements,
grammatically connected, but having no logical coherence.
It is possible that he now and then introduced these more
colloquial paragraphs as a set off to the somewhat exaggerated abruptness and emphasis of his ordinary style.

His more elaborate sentences are carefully constructed
with what musicians would call suspended resolutions; and
differ in this way from what some one terms the flippant

[1] The antithesis, too, is often, as with Lyly, apparent rather
than real.

snip-snap of Macaulay. His style is often harmonious, though it is not worthy to be compared in this respect with the style of Sir Thomas Browne, or with the best prose of Milton. It is often wanting in flexibility, and sometimes in vivacity. But it is always clear, weighty, and vigorous.

IV. CHRONOLOGICAL TABLE OF MILTON'S LIFE.

1608. Born in Bread Street, London (Dec. 9th).
1625. Admitted as pensioner at Christ's College, Cambridge.
1628. Takes his B.A. degree.
1632. Takes his M.A. degree.
1632-8. Life at Horton.
1633 (or 1634). "Arcades" written and acted.
1634. "Comus" performed (Sept. 29th).
1637. His mother dies (April 3rd).
    "Comus" published by Henry Lawes.
1638. "Lycidas" published in the "Justa Edovardo King."
    Milton travels on the Continent.
1639. He returns to England (July or August).
    Lives in St. Bride's Churchyard.
1641. "Of Reformation in England" published.
    "Of Prelatical Episcopacy" published.
    "Animadversions upon the Remonstrant's Defence against Smectymnuus" published.
    "The Reason of Church Government urged against Prelaty" published.
1642. "Apology against a Pamphlet called 'A Modest Confutation of the Animadversions upon the Remonstrant's Defence,'" etc.

1643. Marries Mary Powell (May or June).

" Doctrine and Discipline of Divorce" published (August).

1644. " Of Education. To Master S. Hartlib" published.

"The Judgment of Martin Bucer concerning Divorce" published.

"Areopagitica" published (Nov.).

1645. " Tetrachordon " published (March).

"Colasterion " published (March).

His wife reconciled to him (August). Goes to live in Barbican.

1646. " Poems both English and Latin" published (Jan.).

1647. Death of his father and of his father-in-law. Moves to High Holborn.

1649. " Tenure of Kings and Magistrates " published.

Made Secretary for Foreign Tongues (March).

" Eikonoklastes " published (October).

1651. " Pro Populo Anglicano Defensio contra Salmasium " published.

1652. Becomes totally blind.

His first wife dies.

1654. " Defensio Secunda" published.

1655. " Pro se Defensio contra Morum " published.

1656. Marries Katherine Woodcock.

1658. Death of his second wife.

1659. " Treatise of Civil Power in Ecclesiastical Causes " published.

"Considerations touching the means of removing Hirelings out of the Church" published.

1660. " Ready and Easy Way to Establish a Free Commonwealth" published.

Milton goes into hiding.

1661. Goes to live in Jewin Street, but soon removes to Artillery Walk.

1664. Marries Elizabeth Minshull.
1667. " Paradise Lost " published (April 27th).
1669. " Accidence commenced Grammar " published.
1670. " History of Britain " published.
1671. " Paradise Regained " $\Big\}$ published (in one volume).
     " Samson Agonistes "
1672. " Artis Logicæ Institutio " published.
1673. " Of True Religion, Heresy and Schism " published.
1674. " Epistolarum Familiarum liber " published.
     " Prolusiones Academicæ " published.
     Death of Milton (Nov. 8th).
     Buried at St. Giles, Cripplegate.

V. BOOKS RECOMMENDED.

Bradshaw, " Milton's Poetical Works " (Aldine Poets).

St. John, " Milton's Prose Works," Bohn's edition, Standard Library, five vols.

Masson, " Milton's Poetical Works " (Globe edition), " Life of John Milton," six vols.

Leslie Stephen, article " Milton, John," in the " Dictionary of National Biography," vol. 38.

Garnett, " Life of Milton."

Pattison, " Milton " (English Men of Letters series).

Goodwin, " Lives of Edward and John Philips," which contains Edward Philips' Life of Milton, Aubrey's Life, and other useful material.

Elwood, " History of Thomas Elwood " (Morley's Universal Library).

Jonathan Richardson, " Explanatory Notes on ' Paradise Lost ' " (with Life).

Johnson's " Lives of the Poets," edited by Mrs. Napier ; or Cunningham's edition (out of print).

MILTON.

THE Life of Milton has been already written in so many forms, and with such minute enquiry, that I might perhaps more properly have contented myself with the addition of a few notes to Mr. Fenton's elegant Abridgement, but that a new narrative was thought necessary to the uniformity of this edition.

John Milton was by birth a gentleman, descended from the proprietors of Milton near Thame in Oxfordshire, one of whom forfeited his estate in the times of York and Lancaster. Which side he took I know not; his descendant inherited no veneration for the White Rose.

His grandfather John was keeper of the forest of Shot-over, a zealous papist, who disinherited his son, because he had forsaken the religion of his ancestors.

His father, John, who was the son disinherited, had recourse for his support to the profession of a scrivener. He was a man eminent for his skill in musick, many of his compositions being still to be found; and his reputation in his profession was such, that he grew rich, and retired to an estate. He had probably more than common literature, as his son addresses him in one of his most elaborate Latin poems. He married a gentlewoman of the name of Caston, a Welsh family, by whom he had two sons, John the poet, and Christopher who studied the law, and adhered, as the law taught him, to the King's party, for which he was a while persecuted; but having, by his brother's

B

interest, obtained permission to live in quiet, he supported
himself so honourably by chamber-practice, that soon after
the accession of King James, he was knighted and made a
Judge; but, his constitution being too weak for business,
he retired before any disreputable compliances became
necessary.

He had likewise a daughter Anne, whom he married
with a considerable fortune to Edward Philips, who came
from Shrewsbury, and rose in the Crown-office to be
10 secondary: by him she had two sons, John and Edward,
who were educated by the poet, and from whom is derived
the only authentick account of his domestick manners.

John, the poet, was born in his father's house, at the
"Spread-Eagle" in Bread-street, Dec. 9, 1608, between
six and seven in the morning. His father appears to have
been very solicitous about his education; for he was instructed at first by private tuition under the care of
Thomas Young, who was afterwards chaplain to the English
merchants at Hamburgh; and of whom we have reason to
20 think well, since his scholar considered him as worthy of
an epistolary Elegy.

He was then sent to St. Paul's School, under the care of
Mr. Gill; and removed in the beginning of his sixteenth
year, to Christ's College in Cambridge, where he entered a
sizar, Feb. 12, 1624 (O.S.).

He was at this time eminently skilled in the Latin
tongue; and he himself, by annexing the dates to his first
compositions, a boast of which the learned Politian had
given him an example, seems to commend the earliness of
30 his own proficiency to the notice of posterity. But the
products of his vernal fertility have been surpassed by
many, and particularly by his contemporary Cowley. Of
the powers of the mind it is difficult to form an estimate:
many have excelled Milton in their first essays, who never
rose to works like "Paradise Lost."

At fifteen, a date which he uses till he is sixteen, he translated or versified two Psalms, 114 and 136, which he thought worthy of the publick eye; but they raise no great expectations; they would in any numerous school have obtained praise, but not excited wonder.

Many of his elegies appear to have been written in his eighteenth year, by which it appears that he had then read the Roman authors with very nice discernment. I once heard Mr. Hampton, the translator of "Polybius," remark what I think is true, that Milton was the first English- 10 man who, after the revival of letters, wrote Latin verses with classick elegance. If any exceptions can be made, they are very few: Haddon and Ascham, the pride of Elizabeth's reign, however they may have succeeded in prose, no sooner attempt verses than they provoke derision. If we produced anything worthy of notice before the elegies of Milton, it was perhaps Alabaster's "Roxana."

Of these exercises which the rules of the University required, some were published by him in his maturer 20 years. They had been undoubtedly applauded; for they were such as few can perform: yet there is reason to suspect that he was regarded in his college with no great fondness. That he obtained no fellowship is certain; but the unkindness with which he was treated was not merely negative. I am ashamed to relate what I fear is true, that Milton was one of the last students in either university that suffered the publick indignity of corporal correction.

It was, in the violence of controversial hostility, objected 30 to him, that he was expelled: this he steadily denies, and it was apparently not true; but it seems plain from his own verses to Diodati, that he had incurred Rustication; a temporary dismission into the country, with perhaps the loss of a term:

"Me tenet urbs refluâ quam Thamesis alluit undâ,
  Meque nec patria dulcis habet.
Jam nec arundiferum mihi cura revisere Camum,
  Nec dudum *vetiti* me *laris* angit amor.—
Nec duri libet usque minas perferre magistri,
  Cæteraque ingenio non subeunda meo.
Si sit hoc *exilium* patrias adiisse penates,
  Et vacuum curis otia grata sequi,
Non ego vel *profugi* nomen sortenive recuso,
10 Lœtus et *exilii* conditione fruor."

I cannot find any meaning but this, which even kindness
and reverence can give to the term, *vetiti laris*, " a habitation from which he is excluded ; " or how *exile* can be
otherwise interpreted. He declares yet more, that he is
weary of enduring *the threats of a rigorous master, and
something else, which a temper like his cannot undergo.*
What was more than threat was probably punishment.
This poem, which mentions his *exile*, proves likewise that
it was not perpetual; for it concludes with a resolution of
20 returning some time to Cambridge And it may be conjectured from the willingness with which he has per-
petuated the memory of his exile, that its cause was such
as gave him no shame.

He took both the usual degrees; that of Batchelor in
1628, and that of Master in 1632 ; but he left the university with no kindness for its institution, alienated either
by the injudicious severity of his governors, or his own
captious perverseness. The cause cannot now be known,
but the effect appears in his writings. His scheme of
30 education, inscribed to Hartlib, supersedes all academical
instruction, being intended to comprise the whole time
which men usually spend in literature, from their entrance
upon grammar, *till they proceed, as it is called, masters of
arts.* And in his Discourse " On the likeliest Way to
Remove Hirelings out of the Church," he ingeniously proposes, that *the profits of the lands forfeited by the act for*

superstitious uses, should be applied to such academies all over the land, where languages and arts may be taught together; so that youth may be at once brought up to a competency of learning and an honest trade, by which means such of them as had the gift, being enabled to support themselves (without tithes) by the latter, may, by the help of the former, become worthy preachers.

One of his objections to academical education, as it was then conducted, is, that men designed for orders in the Church were permitted to act plays, *writhing and unboning* 10 *their clergy limbs to all the antick and dishonest gestures of Trinculos, buffoons and bawds, prostituting the shame of that ministry which they had, or were near having, to the eyes of courtiers and court-ladies, their grooms and mademoiselles.*

This is sufficiently peevish in a man, who, when he mentions his exile from the college, relates, with great luxuriance, the compensation which the pleasures of the theatre afford him. Plays were therefore only criminal when they were acted by academicks.

He went to the university with a design of entering into 20 the church, but in time altered his mind; for he declared, that whoever became a clergyman must " subscribe slave, and take an oath withal, which, unless he took with a conscience that could retch, he must straight perjure himself. He thought it better to prefer a blameless silence before the office of speaking, bought and begun with servitude and forswearing."

These expressions are, I find, applied to the subscription of the articles; but it seems more probable that they relate to canonical obedience. I know not any of the Articles 30 which seem to thwart his opinions: but the thoughts of obedience, whether canonical or civil, raised his indignation.

His unwillingness to engage in the ministry, perhaps not yet advanced to a settled resolution of declining it,

appears in a letter to one of his friends, who had reproved
his suspended and dilatory life, which he seems to have
imputed to an insatiable curiosity, and fantastick luxury of
various knowledge.   To this he writes a cool and plausible
answer, in which he endeavors to persuade him that the
delay proceeds not from the delights of desultory study, but
from the desire of obtaining more fitness for his task; and
that he goes on, *not taking thought of being late, so it give
advantage to be more fit.*

10   When he left the university, he returned to his father,
then residing at Horton in Buckinghamshire, with whom
he lived five years; in which time he is said to have read
all the Greek and Latin writers.   With what limitations
this universality is to be understood, who shall inform us ?

It might be supposed that he who read so much
should have done nothing else; but Milton found time to
write the Masque of "Comus," which was presented at
Ludlow, then the residence of the Lord President of Wales,
in 1634; and had the honour of being acted by the Earl
20 of Bridgewater's sons and daughter.   The fiction is derived
from Homer's Circe; but we never can refuse to any
modern the liberty of borrowing from Homer:

> " —a quo ceu fonte perenni
> Vatum Pieriis ora rigantur aquis. "

His next production was " Lycidas," an elegy, written in
1637, on the death of Mr. King, the son of Sir John King,
secretary for Ireland in the time of Elizabeth, James, and
Charles.   King was much a favourite at Cambridge, and
many of the wits joined to do honour to his memory.
30 Milton's acquaintance with the Italian writers may be discovered by a mixture of longer and shorter verses, according
to the rules of Tuscan poetry, and his malignity to the
Church by some lines which are interpreted as threatening
its extermination.

He is supposed about this time to have written his "Arcades;" for while he lived at Horton he used sometimes to steal from his studies a few days, which he spent at Harefield, the house of the countess dowager of Derby, where the "Arcades" made part of a dramatick entertainment.

He began now to grow weary of the country; and had some purpose of taking chambers in the Inns of Court, when the death of his mother set him at liberty to travel, for which he obtained his father's consent, and Sir Henry 10 Wotton's directions, with the celebrated precept of prudence, *i pensieri stretti, ed il viso sciolto;* "thoughts close, and looks loose."

In 1638 he left England, and went first to Paris; where, by the favour of Lord Scudamore, he had the opportunity of visiting Grotius, then residing at the French court as ambassador from Christina of Sweden. From Paris he hasted into Italy, of which he had with particular diligence studied the language and literature: and, though he seems to have intended a very quick perambulation of the country, 20 staid two months at Florence; where he found his way into the academies, and produced his compositions with such applause as appears to have exalted him in his own opinion, and confirmed him in the hope, that, "by labour and intense study, which," says he, "I take to be my portion in this life, joined with a strong propensity of nature," he might "leave something so written to after-times, as they should not willingly let it die."

It appears, in all his writings, that he had the usual concomitant of great abilities, a lofty and steady confidence in 30 himself, perhaps not without some contempt of others; for scarcely any man ever wrote so much, and praised so few. Of his praise he was very frugal; as he set its value high, and considered his mention of a name as a security against the waste of time, and a certain preservative from oblivion.

At Florence he could not indeed complain that his merit wanted distinction. Carlo Dati presented him with an encomiastick inscription, in the tumid lapidary style; and Francini wrote him an ode, of which the first stanza is only empty noise; the rest are perhaps too diffuse on common topicks; but the last is natural and beautiful.

From Florence he went to Sienna, and from Sienna to Rome, where he was again received with kindness by the Learned and the Great. Holstenius, the keeper of the
10 Vatican Library, who had resided three years at Oxford, introduced him to Cardinal Barberini; and he, at a musical entertainment, waited for him at the door, and led him by the hand into the assembly. Here Selvaggi praised him in a distich, and Salsilli in a tetrastick: neither of them of much value. The Italians were gainers by this literary commerce; for the encomiums with which Milton repaid Salsilli, though not secure against a stern grammarian, turn the balance indisputably in Milton's favour.

20 Of these Italian testimonies, poor as they are, he was proud enough to publish them before his poems; though he says, he cannot be suspected but to have known that they were said *non tam de se, quam supra se.*

At Rome, as at Florence, he staid only two months; a time indeed sufficient, if he desired only to ramble with an explainer of its antiquities, or to view palaces and count pictures; but certainly too short for the contemplation of learning, policy, or manners.

From Rome he passed on to Naples, in company of a
30 hermit; a companion from whom little could be expected, yet to him Milton owed his introduction to Manso marquis of Villa, who had been before the patron of Tasso. Manso was enough delighted with his accomplishments to honour him with a sorry distich, in which he commends him for every thing but his religion; and Milton, in return, ad-

dressed him in a Latin poem, which must have raised an high opinion of English elegance and literature.

His purpose was now to have visited Sicily and Greece; but, hearing of the differences between the king and parliament, he thought it proper to hasten home, rather than pass his life in foreign amusements while his countrymen were contending for their rights. He therefore came back to Rome, though the merchants informed him of plots laid against him by the Jesuits, for the liberty of his conversations on religion. He had sense enough to judge that 10 there was no danger, and therefore kept on his way, and acted as before, neither obtruding nor shunning controversy. He had perhaps given some offence by visiting Galileo, then a prisoner in the Inquisition for philosophical heresy; and at Naples he was told by Manso, that, by his declarations on religious questions, he had excluded himself from some distinctions which he should otherwise have paid him. But such conduct, though it did not please, was yet sufficiently safe; and Milton staid two months more at Rome, and went on to Florence without 20 molestation.

From Florence he visited Lucca. He afterwards went to Venice; and having sent away a collection of musick and other books, travelled to Geneva, which he probably considered as the metropolis of orthodoxy. Here he reposed, as in a congenial element, and became acquainted with John Diodati and Frederick Spanheim, two learned professors of Divinity. From Geneva he passed through France; and came home, after an absence of a year and three months.   30

At his return he heard of the death of his friend Charles Diodati; a man whom it is reasonable to suppose of great merit, since he was thought by Milton worthy of a poem, intituled, "Epitaphium Damonis," written with the common but childish imitation of pastoral life.

He now hired a lodging at the house of one Russel, a taylor in St. Bride's Churchyard, and undertook the education of John and Edward Philips, his sister's sons. Finding his rooms too little, he took a house and garden in Aldersgate-street, which was not then so much out of the world as it is now; and chose his dwelling at the upper end of a passage, that he might avoid the noise of the street. Here he received more boys, to be boarded and instructed.

10   Let not our veneration for Milton forbid us to look with some degree of merriment on great promises and small performance, on the man who hastens home, because his countrymen are contending for their liberty, and, when he reaches the scene of action, vapours away his patriotism in a private boarding-school. This is the period of his life from which all his biographers seem inclined to shrink. They are unwilling that Milton should be degraded to a school-master; but, since it cannot be denied that he taught boys, one finds out that he taught for nothing, and
20 another that his motive was only zeal for the propagation of learning and virtue; and all tell what they do not know to be true, only to excuse an act which no wise man will consider as in itself disgraceful. His father was alive; his allowance was not ample; and he supplied its deficiencies by an honest and useful employment.

It is told, that in the art of education he performed wonders; and a formidable list is given of the authors, Greek and Latin, that were read in Aldersgate-street, by youth between ten and fifteen or sixteen years of age.
30 Those who tell or receive these stories should consider that nobody can be taught faster than he can learn. The speed of the horseman must be limited by the power of his horse. Every man, that has ever undertaken to instruct others, can tell what slow advances he has been able to make, and how much patience it requires to recall vagrant inattention,

to stimulate sluggish indifference, and to rectify absurd misapprehension.

The purpose of Milton, as it seems, was to teach something more solid than the common literature of Schools, by reading those authors that treat of physical subjects; such as the " Georgick," and astronomical treatises of the ancients. This was a scheme of improvement which seems to have busied many literary projectors of that age. Cowley, who had more means than Milton of knowing what was wanting to the embellishments of life, formed the same plan of 10 education in his imaginary College.

But the truth is, that the knowledge of external nature, and the sciences which that knowledge requires or includes, are not the great or the frequent business of the human mind. Whether we provide for action or conversation, whether we wish to be useful or pleasing, the first requisite is the religious and moral knowledge of right and wrong ; the next is an aequaintance with the history of mankind, and with those examples which may be said to embody truth, and prove by events the reasonableness of opinions. 20 Prudence and Justice are virtues, and excellences, of all times and of all places ; we are perpetually moralists, but we are geometricians only by chance. Our intercourse with intellectual nature is necessary ; our speculations upon matter are voluntary, and at leisure. Physiological learning is of such rare emergence, that one man may know another half his life without being able to estimate his skill in hydrostaticks or astronomy ; but his moral and prudential character immediately appears.

Those authors, therefore, are to be read at schools 30 that supply most axioms of prudence, most principles of moral truth, and most materials for conversation; and these purposes are best served by poets, orators, and historians.

Let me not be censured for this digression as pedantick or paradoxical; for if I have Milton against me, I have

Socrates on my side. It was his labour to turn philosophy
from the study of nature to speculations upon life; but
the innovators whom I oppose are turning off attention
from life to nature.   They seem to think, that we are
placed here to watch the growth of plants, or the motions
of the stars.   Socrates was rather of opinion, that what
we had to learn was, how to do good, and avoid evil.

Οττι τοι ἐν μεγάροισι κακόντ' ἀγαθόντε τέτυκται.

Of institutions we may judge by their effects.   From
10 this wonder-working academy, I do not know that there
ever proceeded any man very eminent for knowledge : its
only genuine product, I believe, is a small History of
Poetry, written in Latin by his nephew Philips, of which
perhaps none of my readers has ever heard.

That in his school, as in every thing else which he
undertook, he laboured with great diligence, there is no
reason for doubting.   One part of his method deserves
general imitation.   He was careful to instruct his scholars
in religion.   Every Sunday was spent upon theology, of which
20 he dictated a short system, gathered from the writers that
were then fashionable in the Dutch universities.

He set his pupils an example of hard study and spare diet;
only now and then he allowed himself to pass a day of festivity and indulgence with some gay gentlemen of Gray's Inn.
He now began to engage in the controversies of the
times, and lent his breath to blow the flames of contention.
In 1641 he published a treatise of "Reformation," in two
books, against the established Church ; being willing to
help the Puritans, who were, he says, *inferior to the Prelates*
30 *in learning*.

Hall bishop of Norwich had published an "Humble Remonstrance," in defence of Episcopacy; to which, in 1641,
six ministers, of whose names the first letters made the
celebrated word *Smectymnuus*, gave their Answer.   Of this

answer a Confutation was attempted by the learned Usher; and to the Confutation Milton published a Reply, intituled, " Of Prelatical Episcopacy, and whether it may be deduced from the Apostolical Times, by virtue of those testimonies which are alledged to that purpose in some late treatises, one whereof goes under the name of James Lord Bishop of Armagh."

I have transcribed this title, to shew, by his contemptuous mention of Usher, that he had now adopted the puritanical savageness of manners. His next work was, 10 "The Reason of Church Government urged against Prelacy, by Mr. John Milton," 1642. In this book he discovers, not with ostentatious exultation, but with calm confidence, his high opinion of his own powers; and promises to undertake something, he yet knows not what, that may be of use and honour to his country. "This," says he, "is not to be obtained but by devout prayer to that Eternal Spirit that can enrich with all utterance and knowledge, and sends out his Seraphim with the hallowed fire of his altar, to touch and purify the lips of whom he pleases. To this 20 must be added, industrious and select reading, steady observation, and insight into all seemly and generous arts and affairs; till which in some measure be compast, I refuse not to sustain this expectation." From a promise like this, at once fervid, pious, and rational, might be expected the " Paradise Lost."

He published the same year two more pamphlets, upon the same question. To one of his antagonists, who affirms that he was *vomited out of the university*, he answers, in general terms; " The Fellows of the College wherein I 30 spent some years, at my parting, after I had taken two degrees, as the manner is, signified many times how much better it would content them that I should stay.—As for the common approbation or dislike of that place, as now it is, that I should esteem or disesteem myself the more

for that, too simple is the answerer, if he think to obtain with me. Of small practice were the physician who could not judge, by what she and her sister have of long time vomited, that the worser stuff she strongly keeps in her stomach, but the better she is ever kecking at, and is queasy: she vomits now out of sickness; but before it be well with her, she must vomit by strong physick.—The university, in the time of her better health, and my younger judgement, I never greatly admired, but. now
10 much less."

This is surely the language of a man who thinks that he has been injured. He proceeds to describe the course of his conduct, and the train of his thoughts; and, because he has been suspected of incontinence, gives an account of his own purity: "That if I be justly charged," says he, "with this crime, it may come upon me with tenfold shame."

The style of his piece is rough, and such perhaps was that of his antagonist. This roughness he justifies, by
20 great examples, in a long digression. Sometimes he tries to be humorous: "Lest I should take him for some chaplain in hand, some squire of the body to his prelate, one who serves not at the altar only but at the Court-cupboard, he will bestow on us a pretty model of himself; and sets me out half a dozen ptisical mottos, wherever he had them, hopping short in the measure of convulsion fits; in which labour the agony of his wit having scaped narrowly, instead of well-sized periods, he greets us with a quantity of thumbring posies.—And thus ends this section,
30 or rather dissection of himself." Such is the controversial merriment of Milton; his gloomy seriousness is yet more offensive. Such is his malignity, *that hell grows darker at his frown.*

His father, after Reading was taken by Essex, came to reside in his house; and his school increased. At Whit-

suntide, in his thirty-fifth year, he married Mary, the
daughter of Mr. Powel, a justice of the Peace in Oxfordshire. He brought her to town with him, and expected all
the advantages of a conjugal life. The lady, however,
seems not much to have delighted in the pleasures of
spare diet and hard study; for, as Philips relates, "having
for a month led a philosophical life, after having been
used at home to a great house, and much company and
joviality, her friends, possibly by her own desire, made
earnest suit to have her company the remaining part of the 10
summer; which was granted, upon a promise of her return
at Michaelmas."

Milton was too busy to much miss his wife: he pursued
his studies; and now and then visited the Lady Margaret
Leigh, whom he has mentioned in one of his sonnets. At
last Michaelmas arrived; but the Lady had no inclination
to return to the sullen gloom of her husband's habitation,
and therefore very willingly forgot her promise. He sent
her a letter, but had no answer; he sent more with the
same success. It could be alleged that letters miscarry; 20
he therefore dispatched a messenger, being by this time too
angry to go himself. His messenger was sent back with
some contempt. The family of the Lady were Cavaliers.

In a man whose opinion of his own merit was like
Milton's, less provocation than this might have raised
violent resentment. Milton soon determined to repudiate
her for disobedience; and, being one of those who could
easily find arguments to justify inclination, published (in
1644) "The Doctrine and Discipline of Divorce;" which
was followed by "The Judgement of Martin Bucer, con- 30
cerning Divorce;" and the next year, his "Tetrachordon,
Expositions upon the four chief Places of Scripture which
treat of Marriage."

This innovation was opposed, as might be expected, by
the clergy; who, then holding their famous assembly at

Westminster, procured· that the author should be called
before the Lords; "but that House," says Wood, "whether
approving the doctrine, or not favouring his accusers, did
soon dismiss him."

There seems not to have been much written against him,
nor any thing by any writer of eminence.   The antagonist
that appeared is styled by him, "A Serving man turned
Solicitor." Howel in his letters mentions the new doctrine
with contempt; and it was, I suppose, thought more
10 worthy of derision than of confutation.   He complains of
this neglect in two sonnets, of which the first is con-
temptible, and the second not excellent.

From this time it is observed that he became an enemy
to the Presbyterians, whom he had favoured before.   He
that changes his party by his humour, is not more virtuous
than he that changes it by his interest; he loves himself
rather than truth.

His wife and her relations now found that Milton was
not an unresisting sufferer of injuries; and perceiving that
20 he had begun to put his doctrine in practice, by courting a
young woman of great accomplishments, the daughter of
one Doctor Davis, who was however not ready to comply,
they resolved to endeavour a re-union. He went sometimes
to the house of one Blackborough, his relation, in the lane
of St. Martin's-le-Grand, and at one of his usual visits was
surprised to see his wife come from another room, and
implore forgiveness on her knees. He resisted her intreaties
for a while; "but partly," says Philips, "his own generous
nature, more inclinable to reconciliation than to perse-
30 verance in anger or revenge, and partly the strong inter-
cession of friends on both sides, soon brought him to an
act of oblivion and a firm league of peace." It were in-
jurious to omit, that Milton afterwards received her father
and her brothers in his own house, when they were distressed, with other Royalists.

He published about the same time his "Areopagitica, a Speech of Mr. John Milton for the liberty of unlicensed Printing." The danger of such unbounded liberty, and the danger of bounding it, have produced a problem in the science of Government, which human understanding seems hitherto unable to solve. If nothing may be published but what civil authority shall have previously approved, power must always be the standard of truth; if every dreamer of innovations may propagate his projects, there can be no settlement; if every murmurer at government 10 may diffuse discontent, there can be no peace; and if every sceptick in theology may teach his follies, there can be no religion. The remedy against these evils is to punish the authors; for it is yet allowed that every society may punish, though not prevent, the publication of opinions, which that society shall think pernicious; but this punishment, though it may crush the author, promotes the book; and it seems not more reasonable to leave the right of printing unrestrained, because writers may be afterwards censured, than it would be to sleep with doors unbolted, 20 because by our laws we can hang a thief.

But whatever were his engagements, civil or domestick, poetry was never long out of his thoughts. About this time (1645) a collection of his Latin and English poems appeared, in which the "Allegro" and "Penseroso," with some others, were first published.

He had taken a larger house in Barbican for the reception of scholars; but the numerous relations of his wife, to whom he generously granted refuge for a while, occupied his rooms. In time, however, they went away; "and the 30 house again," says Philips, "now looked like a house of the Muses only, though the accession of scholars was not great. Possibly his having proceeded so far in the education of youth, may have been the occasion of his adversaries calling him pedagogue and school-master; whereas it is

c

well known he never set up for a publick school, to teach
all the young fry of a parish; but only was willing to im-
part his learning and knowledge to relations, and the sons
of gentlemen who were his intimate friends; and that
neither his writings nor his way of teaching ever savoured
in the least of pedantry."

Thus laboriously does his nephew extenuate what cannot
be denied, and what might be confessed without disgrace.
Milton was not a man who could become mean by a mean
10 employment. This, however, his warmest friends seem not
to have found; they therefore shift and palliate. He did
not sell literature to all comers at an open shop; he was a
chamber-milliner, and measured his commodities only to
his friends.

Philips, evidently impatient of viewing him in this state
of degradation, tells us that it was not long continued;
and, to raise his character again, has a mind to invest him
with military splendour: "He is much mistaken," he says,
"if there was not about this time a design of making him
20 an adjutant-general in Sir William Waller's army. But
the new modelling of the army proved an obstruction to
the design." An event cannot be set at a much greater
distance than by having been only *designed, about some
time*, if a man *be not much mistaken*. Milton shall be a
pedagogue no longer; for, if Philips be not much mistaken,
somebody at some time designed him for a soldier.

About the time that the army was new-modelled (1645)
he removed to a smaller house in Holbourn, which opened
backward into Lincoln's-Inn-Fields. He is not known to
30 have published any thing afterwards till the King's death,
when, finding his murderers condemned by the Presbyterians, he wrote a treatise to justify it, and *to compose the
minds of the people*.

He made some "Remarks on the Articles of Peace between Ormond and the Irish Rebels." While he contented

himself to write, he perhaps did only what his conscience dictated; and if he did not very vigilantly watch the influence of his own passions, and the gradual prevalence of opinions, first willingly admitted and then habitually indulged, if objections, by being overlooked, were forgotten, and desire superinduced conviction; he yet shared only the common weakness of mankind, and might be no less sincere than his opponents. But as faction seldom leaves a man honest, however it might find him, Milton is suspected of having interpolated the book called "Icon Basi- 10 like," which the Council of State, to whom he was now made Latin secretary, employed him to censure, by inserting a prayer taken from Sidney's "Arcadia," and imputing it to the King; whom he charges, in his "Iconoclastes," with the use of this prayer as with a heavy crime, in the indecent language with which prosperity had emboldened the advocates for rebellion to insult all that is venerable or great: "Who would have imagined so little fear in him of the true all-seeing Deity—as, immediately before his death, to pop into the hands of the grave bishop that attended 20 him, as a special relique of his saintly exercises, a prayer stolen word for word from the mouth of a heathen woman praying to a heathen god?"

The papers which the King gave to Dr. Juxon on the scaffold the regicides took away, so that they were at least the publishers of this prayer; and Dr. Birch, who had examined the question with great care, was inclined to think them the forgers. The use of it by adaptation was innocent; and they who could so noisily censure it, with a little extension of their malice could contrive what they 30 wanted to accuse.

King Charles the Second, being now sheltered in Holland, employed Salmasius, professor of Polite Learning at Leyden, to write a defence of his father and of monarchy; and, to excite his industry, gave him, as was reported, a

hundred Jacobuses. Salmasius was a man of skill in languages, knowledge of antiquity, and sagacity of emenda-
tory criticism, almost exceeding all hope of human attain-
ment; and having, by excessive praises, been confirmed in
great confidence of himself, though he probably had not
much considered the principles of society or the rights of
government, undertook the employment without distrust of
his own qualifications; and, as his expedition in writing
was wonderful, in 1649 published " Defensio Regis."

10   To this Milton was required to write a sufficient answer;
which he performed (1651) in such a manner, that Hobbes
declared himself unable to decide whose language was
best, or whose arguments were worst. In my opinion,
Milton's periods are smoother, neater, and more pointed;
but he delights himself with teizing his adversary as much
as with confuting him. He makes a foolish allusion of
Salmasius, whose doctrine he considers as servile and un-
manly, to the stream of " Salmacis," which whoever entered
left half his virility behind him. Salmasius was a French-
20 man, and was unhappily married to a scold. *Tu es Gallus,*
says Milton, *et, ut aiunt, nimium gallinaceus.* But his
supreme pleasure is to tax his adversary, so renowned
for criticism, with vitious Latin. He opens his book with
telling that he has used *Persona,* which, according to
Milton, signifies only a *Mask,* in a sense not known to the
Romans, by applying it as we apply *Person.* But as
Nemesis is always on the watch, it is memorable that he
· has enforced the charge of a solecism by an expression in
itself grossly solecistical, when, for one of those supposed
30 blunders, he says, as Ker, and I think some one before
him, has remarked, *propino te grammatistis tuis* vapulan-
dum. From *vapulo,* which has a passive sense, *vapulandus*
can never be derived. No man forgets his original trade:
the rights of nations, and of kings, sink into questions of
grammar, if grammarians discuss them.

Milton when he undertook this answer was weak of body, and dim of sight; but his will was forward, and what was wanting of health was supplied by zeal. He was rewarded by a thousand pounds, and his book was much read; for paradox, recommended by spirit and elegance, easily gains attention; and he who told every man that he was equal to his King, could hardly want an audience.

That the performance of Salmasius was not dispersed with equal rapidity, or read with equal eagerness, is very credible. He taught only the stale doctrine of authority, 10 and the unpleasing duty of submission; and he had been so long not only the monarch but the tyrant of literature, that almost all mankind were delighted to find him defied and insulted by a new name, not yet considered as any one's rival. If Christina, as is said, commended the "Defence of the People," her purpose must be to torment Salmasius, who was then at her Court; for neither her civil station nor her natural character could dispose her to favour the doctrine, who was by birth a queen, and by temper despotick. 20

That Salmasius was, from the appearance of Milton's book, treated with neglect, there is not much proof; but to a man so long accustomed to admiration, a little praise of his antagonist would be sufficiently offensive, and might incline him to leave Sweden, from which, however, he was dismissed, not with any mark of contempt, but with a train of attendance scarce less than regal.

He prepared a reply, which, left as it was imperfect, was published by his son in the year of the Restauration. In the beginning, being probably most in pain for his Latinity, 30 he endeavours to defend his use of the word *persona*; but, if I remember right, he misses a better authority than any that he has found, that of Juvenal in his fourth satire:

> "—Quid agis cum dira & fœdior omni
> Crimine *Persona* est?"

As Salmasius reproached Milton with losing his eyes in
the quarrel, Milton delighted himself with the belief that
he had shortened Salmasius's life, and both perhaps with
more malignity than reason. Salmasius died at the Spa,
Sept. 3, 1653 ; and as controvertists are commonly said to
be killed by their last dispute, Milton was flattered with
the credit of destroying him.

Cromwell had now dismissed the parliament by the
authority of which he had destroyed monarchy, and com-
10 menced monarch himself, under the title of protector, but
with kingly and more than kingly power. That his authority was lawful, never was pretended ; he himself founded
his right only in necessity ; but Milton, having now tasted
the honey of publick employment, would not return to
hunger and philosophy, but, continuing to exercise his
office under a manifest usurpation, betrayed to his power
that liberty which he had defended. Nothing can be more
just than that rebellion should end in slavery ; that he,
who had justified the murder of his king, for some acts
20 which to him seemed unlawful, should now sell his services, and his flatteries, to a tyrant, of whom it was evident
that he could do nothing lawful.

He had now been blind for some years ; but his vigour
of intellect was such, that he was not disabled to discharge
his office of Latin secretary, or continue his controversies.
His mind was too eager to be diverted, and too strong to
be subdued.

About this time his first wife died in childbed, having
left him three daughters. As he probably did not much love
30 her, he did not long continue the appearance of lamenting
her ; but after a short time married Catherine, the daughter
of one captain Woodcock of Hackney ; a woman doubtless
educated in opinions like his own. She died within a year,
of childbirth, or some distemper that followed it ; and her
husband has honoured her memory with a poor sonnet.

The first Reply to Milton's "Defensio Populi" was published in 1651, called "Apologia pro Rege & Populo Anglicano, contra Johannis Polypragmatici (alias Miltoni) defensionem destructivam Regis & Populi." Of this the author was not known; but Milton and his nephew Philips, under whose name he published an answer so much corrected by him that it might be called his own, imputed it to Bramhal; and, knowing him no friend to regicides, thought themselves at liberty to treat him as if they had known what they only suspected. 10

Next year appeared "Regii Sanguinis clamor ad Cœlum." Of this the author was Peter du Moulin, who was afterwards prebendary of Canterbury; but Morus, or More, a French minister, having the care of its publication, was treated as the writer by Milton in his "Defensio Secunda," and overwhelmed by such violence of invective, that he began to shrink under the tempest, and gave his persecutors the means of knowing the true author. Du Moulin was now in great danger; but Milton's pride operated against his malignity; and both he and his friends were more willing 20 that Du Moulin should escape than that he should be convicted of mistake.

In this second Defence he shews that his eloquence is not merely satirical; the rudeness of his invective is equalled by the grossness of his flattery. "Deserimur, Cromuelle, tu solis superes, ad te summa nostrarum rerum rediit, in te solo consistit, insuperabili tuæ virtuti cedimus cuncti, nemine vel obloquente, nisi qui æquales inæqualis ipse honores sibi quærit, aut digniori concessos invidet, aut non intelligit nihil esse in societate hominum magis vel 30 Deo gratum, vel rationi consentaneum, esse in civitate nihil æquius, nihil utilius, quam potiri rerum dignissimum. Eum te agnoscunt omnes, Cromuelle, ea tu civis maximus et gloriosissimus, dux publici consilii, exercituum fortissimorum imperator, pater patriæ gessisti. Sic tu spontanea bonorum omnium et animitus missa voce salutaris."

Cæsar, when he assumed the perpetual dictatorship, had not more servile or more elegant flattery. A translation may shew its servility; but its elegance is less attainable. Having exposed the unskilfulness or selfishness of the former government, "We were left," says Milton, "to ourselves: the whole national interest fell into your hands, and subsists only in your abilities. To your virtue, over-
10 powering and resistless, every man gives way, except some who, without equal qualifications, aspire to equal honours, who envy the distinctions of merit greater than their own, or who have yet to learn, that in the coalition of human society nothing is more pleasing to God, or more agreeable to reason, than that the highest mind should have the sovereign power. Such, Sir, are you by general confession; such are the things atchieved by you, the greatest and most glorious of our countrymen, the director of our publick councils, the leader of unconquered armies, the father of
20 your country; for by that title does every good man hail you, with sincere and voluntary praise."

Next year, having defended all that wanted defence, he found leisure to defend himself. He undertook his own vindication against More, whom he declares in his title to be justly called the author of the "Regii Sanguinis clamor." In this there is no want of vehemence nor eloquence, nor does he forget his wonted wit. "Morus es? an Momus? an uterque idem est?" He then remembers that *Morus* is Latin for a Mulberry-tree, and hints at the known
30 transformation:

> " —Poma alba ferebat
> Quæ post nigra tulit Morus."

With this piece ended his controversies; and he from this time gave himself up to his private studies and his civil employment.

As secretary to the Protector he is supposed to have written the Declaration of the reasons for a war with Spain. His agency was considered as of great importance; for when a treaty with Sweden was artfully suspended, the delay was publickly imputed to Mr. Milton's indisposition; and the Swedish agent was provoked to express his wonder, that only one man in England could write Latin, and that man blind.

Being now forty-seven years old, and seeing himself disencumbered from external interruptions, he seems to 10 have recollected his former purposes, and to have resumed three great works which he had planned for his future employment: an epick poem, the history of his country, and a dictionary of the Latin tongue.

To collect a dictionary, seems a work of all others least practicable in a state of blindness, because it depends upon perpetual and minute inspection and collation. Nor would Milton probably have begun it, after he had lost his eyes; but, having had it always before him, he continued it, says Philips, *almost to his dying-day; but the papers were so* 20 *discomposed and deficient, that they could not be fitted for the press.* The compilers of the Latin dictionary, printed at Cambridge, had the use of those collections in three folios; but what was their fate afterwards is not known.

To compile a history from various authors, when they can only be consulted by other eyes, is not easy, nor possible, but with more skilful and attentive help than can be commonly obtained; and it was probably the difficulty of consulting and comparing that stopped Milton's narrative at the Conquest; a period at which affairs were not yet very 30 intricate, nor authors very numerous.

For the subject of his epick poem, after much deliberation, *long chusing, and beginning late,* he fixed upon "Paradise Lost;" a design so comprehensive, that it could be justified only by success. He had once designed to cele-

brate King Arthur, as he hints in his verses to Mansus;
but *Arthur was reserved*, says Fenton, *to another destiny.*

It appears, by some sketches of poetical projects left in
manuscript, and to be seen in a library at Cambridge, that
he had digested his thoughts on this subject into one of
those wild dramas which were anciently called Mysteries;
and Philips had seen what he terms part of a tragedy, beginning with the first ten lines of Satan's address to the
Sun. These Mysteries consist of allegorical persons; such
10 as *Justice, Mercy, Faith.* Of the tragedy or mystery of
" Paradise Lost " there are two plans:

The Persons.	The Persons.
Michael.	Moses.
Chorus of Angels.	Divine Justice, Wisdom,
Heavenly Love.	Heavenly Love.
Lucifer.	The Evening Star, Hesperus.
Adam, } with the Serpent.	Chorus of Angels.
Eve,	Lucifer.
Conscience.	Adam.
20 Death,	Eve.
Labour,	Conscience.
Sickness,	Labour,
Discontent, }Mutes.	Sickness,
Ignorance,	Discontent, }Mutes.
with others;	Ignorance,
Faith.	Fear,
Hope.	Death.
Charity.	Faith.
	Hope.
30	Charity.

Paradise Lost.

The Persons.

Moses, προλογίζει, recounting how he assumed his true

body; that it corrupts not, because it is with God in the
mount; declares the like of Enoch and Elijah; besides
the purity of the place, that certain pure winds, dews, and
clouds, preserves it from corruption; whence exhorts to the
sight of God; tells, they cannot see Adam in the state of
innocence, by reason of their sin.

Justice,
Mercy, } debating what should become of man, if he fall.
Wisdom,
Chorus of Angels singing a hymn of the Creation.   10

ACT II.

Heavenly Love.
Evening Star.
Chorus sing the marriage-song, and describe Paradise.

ACT III.

Lucifer, contriving Adam's ruin.
Chorus fears for Adam, and relates Lucifer's rebellion and
    fall.

ACT IV.

Adam, } fallen.   20
Eve,
Conscience cites them to God's examination.
Chorus bewails, and tells the good Adam has lost.

ACT V.

Adam and Eve driven out of Paradise.
—— — —— presented by an angel with
Labour, Grief, Hatred, Envy, War, Famine,
    Pestilence, Sickness, Discontent, Ignorance, } Mutes.
    Fear, Death,

To whom he gives their names. Likewise Winter, Heat, Tempest,

Faith,
Hope,   } comfort and instruct him.
Charity,
Chorus briefly concludes.

Such was his first design, which could have produced only an allegory, or mystery. The following sketch seems to have attained more maturity.

10   " Adam unparadised:

The angel Gabriel, either descending or entering; shew-
· ing, since this globe was created, his frequency as much on earth as in heaven; describes Paradise. Next, the Chorus, shewing the reason of his coming to keep his watch in Paradise, after Lucifer's rebellion, by command from God; and withal expressing his desire to see and know more concerning this excellent new creature, man. The angel Gabriel, as by his name signifying a prince of power, tracing Paradise with a more free office, passes by the 20 station of the Chorus, and, desired by them, relates what he knew of man; as the creation of Eve, with their love and marriage. After this, Lucifer appears; after his over-throw, bemoans himself, seeks revenge on man. The Chorus prepare resistance at his first approach. At last, after discourse of enmity on either side, he departs: whereat the Chorus sings of the battle and victory in heaven, against him and his accomplices: as before, after the first act, was sung a hymn of the creation. Here again may appear Lucifer, relating and insulting in what he had 30 done to the destruction of man. Man next, and Eve having by this time been seduced by the Serpent, appears confusedly covered with leaves. Conscience, in a shape, accuses him; Justice cites him to the place whither Jeho-

vah called for him. In the mean while, the Chorus entertains the stage, and is informed by some angel the manner
of the Fall. Here the Chorus bewails Adam's fall; Adam
then and Eve return; accuse one another; but especially
Adam lays the blame to his wife; is stubborn in his
offence. Justice appears, reasons with him, convinces him.
The Chorus admonisheth Adam, and bids him beware
Lucifer's example of impenitence. The angel is sent to
banish them out of Paradise; but before causes to pass
before his eyes, in shapes, a mask of all the evils of this 10
life and world. He is humbled, relents, despairs: at last
appears Mercy, comforts him, promises the Messiah; then
calls in Faith, Hope, and Charity; instructs him; he re-
pents, gives God the glory, submits to his penalty. The
Chorus briefly concludes. Compare this with the former
draught."

These are very imperfect rudiments of "Paradise Lost;"
but it is pleasant to see great works in their seminal state,
pregnant with latent possibilities of excellence; nor could
there be any more delightful entertainment than to trace 20
their gradual growth and expansion, and to observe how
they are sometimes suddenly advanced by accidental hints,
and sometimes slowly improved by steady meditation.

Invention is almost the only literary labour which blindness cannot obstruct, and therefore he naturally solaced his
solitude by the indulgence of his fancy, and the melody of
his numbers. He had done what he knew to be necessarily previous to poetical excellence; he had made himself
acquainted with *seemly arts and affairs;* his comprehen-
sion was extended by various knowledge, and his memory 30
stored with intellectual treasures. He was skilful in many
languages, and had by reading and composition attained
the full mastery of his own. He would have wanted little
help from books, had he retained the power of perusing
them.

But while his greater designs were advancing, having now, like many other authors, caught the love of publication, he amused himself, as he could, with little productions. He sent to the press (1658) a manuscript of Raleigh, called the "Cabinet Council;" and next year gratified his malevolence to the clergy, by a "Treatise of Civil Power in Ecclesiastical Cases," and "The Means of removing Hirelings out of the Church."

Oliver was now dead; Richard was constrained to re-
10 sign: the system of extemporary government, which had been held together only by force, naturally fell into fragments when that force was taken away; and Milton saw himself and his cause in equal danger. But he had still hope of doing something. He wrote letters, which Toland has published, to such men as he thought friends to the new commonwealth; and even in the year of the Restoration he *he bated no jot of heart or hope*, but was fantastical enough to think that the nation, agitated as it was, might be settled by a pamphlet, called "A ready and easy way
20 to establish a Free Commonwealth;" which was, however, enough considered to be both seriously and ludicrously answered.

The obstinate enthusiasm of the commonwealthmen was very remarkable. When the King was apparently returning, Harrington, with a few associates as fanatical as himself, used to meet, with all the gravity of political importance, to settle an equal government by rotation; and Milton, kicking when he could strike no longer, was foolish enough to publish, a few weeks before the Restoration, *Notes* upon
30 a sermon preached by one Griffiths, intituled, "The Fear of God and the King." To these notes an answer was written by L'Estrange, in a pamphlet petulantly called "No blind Guides."

But whatever Milton could write, or men of greater activity could do, the King was now about to be restored

with the irresistible approbation of the people. He was
therefore no longer secretary, and was consequently obliged
to quit the house which he held by his office; and propor-
tioning his sense of danger to his opinion of the importance
of his writings, thought it convenient to seek some shelter,
and hid himself for a time in Bartholomew-Close by West
Smithfield.

I cannot but remark a kind of respect, perhaps uncon-
sciously, paid to this great man by his biographers: every
house in which he resided is historically mentioned, as if 10
it were an injury to neglect naming any place that he
honoured by his presence.

The King, with lenity of which the world has had perhaps no other example, declined to be the judge or avenger
of his own or his father's wrongs; and promised to admit
into the Act of Oblivion all, except those whom the parliament should except; and the parliament doomed none to
capital punishment but the wretches who had immediately
co-operated in the murder of the King. Milton was certainly not one of them; he had only justified what they 20
had done.

This justification was indeed sufficiently offensive; and
(June 16) an order was issued to seize Milton's "Defence,"
and Goodwin's "Obstructors of Justice," another book of
the same tendency, and burn them by the common hangman. The attorney-general was ordered to prosecute the
authors; but Milton was not seized, nor perhaps very
diligently pursued.

Not long after (August 19) the flutter of innumerable
bosoms was stilled by an act, which the King, that his 30
mercy might want no recommendation of elegance, rather
called an *act of oblivion* than of grace. Goodwin was
named, with nineteen more, as incapacitated for any publick trust; but of Milton there was no exception.

Of this tenderness shewn to Milton, the curiosity of

mankind has not forborn to enquire the reason. Burnet
thinks he was forgotten; but this is another instance
which may confirm Dalrymple's observation, who says,
"that whenever Burnet's narrations are examined, he
appears to be mistaken."

Forgotten he was not; for his prosecution was ordered;
it must be therefore by design that he was included in the
general oblivion. He is said to have had friends in the
House, such as Marvel, Morrice, and Sir Thomas Clarges;
10 and undoubtedly a man like him must have had influence.
A very particular story of his escape is told by Richardson
in his Memoirs, which he received from Pope, as delivered
by Betterton, who might have heard it from Davenant.
In the war between the King and Parliament, Davenant
was made prisoner, and condemned to die; but was spared
at the request of Milton. When the turn of success
brought Milton into the like danger, Davenant repaid the
benefit by appearing in his favour. Here is a reciprocation
of generosity and gratitude so pleasing, that the tale makes
20 its own way to credit. But if help were wanted, I know
not where to find it. The danger of Davenant is certain
from his own relation; but of his escape there is no account. Betterton's narration can be traced no higher; it
is not known that he had it from Davenant. We are told
that the benefit exchanged was life for life; but it seems
not certain that Milton's life ever was in danger. Goodwin, who had committed the same kind of crime, escaped
with incapacitation; and as exclusion from publick trust
is a punishment which the power of government can com-
30 monly inflict without the help of a particular law, it required no great interest to exempt Milton from a censure
little more than verbal. Something may be reasonably
ascribed to veneration and compassion; to veneration of
his abilities, and compassion for his distresses, which
made it fit to forgive his malice for his learning. He was

now poor and blind; and who would pursue with violence
an illustrious enemy, depressed by fortune, and disarmed
by nature?

The publication of the act of oblivion put him in the
same condition with his fellow-subjects. He was, however,
upon some pretence not now known, in the custody of the
serjeant in December; and, when he was released, upon
his refusal of the fees demanded, he and the serjeant were
called before the House. He was now safe within the
shade of oblivion, and knew himself to be as much out of 10
the power of a griping officer as any other man. How the
question was determined is not known. Milton would
hardly have contended, but that he knew himself to have
right on his side.

He then removed to Jewin-street, near Aldersgate-
street; and being blind, and by no means wealthy, wanted
a domestick companion and attendant; and therefore,
by the recommendation of Dr. Paget, married Elizabeth
Minshul, of a gentleman's family in Cheshire, probably
without a fortune. All his wives were virgins; for he 20
has declared that he thought it gross and indelicate to
be a second husband: upon what other principles his
choice was made, cannot now be known; but marriage
afforded not much of his happiness. The first wife left
him in disgust, and was brought back only by terror;
the second, indeed, seems to have been more a favourite,
but her life was short. The third, as Philips relates,
oppressed his children in his life-time, and cheated them
at his death.

Soon after his marriage, according to an obscure story, 30
he was offered the continuance of his employment; and,
being pressed by his wife to accept it, answered, "You,
like other women, want to ride in your coach; my wish is
to live and die an honest man." If he considered the
Latin secretary as exercising any of the powers of govern-

ment, he that had shared authority either with the parliament or Cromwell, might have forborn to talk very loudly of his honesty ; and if he thought the office purely ministerial, he certainly might have honestly retained it under the king.   But this tale has too little evidence to deserve a disquisition ; large offers and sturdy rejections are among the most common topicks of falsehood.

He had so much either of prudence or gratitude, that he forbore to disturb the new settlement with any of his
10 political or ecclesiastical opinions, and from this time devoted himself to poetry and literature.   Of his zeal for learning, in all its parts, he gave a proof by publishing, the next year (1661), " Accidence commenced Grammar ; " a little book which has nothing remarkable, but that its author, who had been lately defending the supreme powers of his country, and was then writing " Paradise Lost," could descend from his elevation to rescue children from the perplexity of grammatical confusion, and the trouble of lessons unnecessarily repeated.

20   About this time Elwood the quaker, being recommended to him as one who would read Latin to him, for the advantage of his conversation; attended him every afternoon, except on Sundays.   Milton, who, in his letter to Hartlib, had declared, that *to read Latin with an English mouth is as ill a hearing as Law French*, required that Elwood should learn and practise the Italian pronunciation, which, he said, was necessary, if he would talk with foreigners. This seems to have been a task troublesome without use. There is little reason for preferring the Italian pronuncia-
30 tion to our own, except that it is more general; and to teach it to an Englishman is only to make him a foreigner at home.   He who travels, if he speaks Latin, may so soon learn the sounds which every native gives it, that he need make no provision before his journey; and if strangers visit us, it is their business to practise such conformity to

our modes as they expect from us in their own countries.
Elwood complied with the directions, and improved himself
by his attendance; for he relates, that Milton, having a
curious ear, knew by his voice when he read what he did
not understand, and would stop him, and *open the most
difficult passages.*

In a short time he took a house in the *Artillery Walk*,
leading to *Bunhill Fields ;* the mention of which concludes
the register of Milton's removals and habitations. He
lived longer in this place than in any other.   10

He was now busied by "Paradise Lost." Whence he
drew the original design has been variously conjectured,
by men who cannot bear to think themselves ignorant of
that which, at last, neither diligence nor sagacity can discover. Some find the hint in an Italian tragedy. Voltaire
tells a wild and unauthorised story of a farce seen by
Milton in Italy, which opened thus : *Let the Rainbow be
the Fiddlestick of the Fiddle of Heaven.* It has been already
shewn, that the first conception was a tragedy or mystery,
not of a narrative, but a dramatick work, which he is sup- 20
posed to have begun to reduce to its present form about
the time (1655) when he finished his dispute with the
defenders of the king.

He long before had promised to adorn his native country
by some great performance, while he had yet perhaps no
settled design, and was stimulated only by such expectations as naturally arose from the survey of his attainments,
and the consciousness of his powers. What he should
undertake, it was difficult to determine. He was *long
chusing, and began late.*   30

While he was obliged to divide his time between his
private studies and affairs of state, his poetical labour must
have been often interrupted ; and perhaps he did little
more in that busy time than construct the narrative, adjust
the episodes, proportion the parts, accumulate images and

sentiments, and treasure in his memory, or preserve in writing, such hints as books or meditation would supply. Nothing particular is known of his intellectual operations while he was a statesman; for, having every help and accommodation at hand, he had no need of uncommon expedients.

Being driven from all publick stations, he is yet too great not to be traced by curiosity to his retirement; where he has been found by Mr. Richardson, the fondest
10 of his admirers, sitting *before his door in a grey coat of coarse cloth, in warm sultry weather, to enjoy the fresh air; and so, as well as in his own room, receiving the visits of people of distinguished parts as well as quality.* His visitors of high quality must now be imagined to be few; but men of parts might reasonably court the conversation of a man so generally illustrious, that foreigners are reported, by Wood, to have visited the house in Bread-street where he was born.

According to another account, he was seen in a small
20 house, *neatly enough dressed in black cloaths, sitting in a room hung with rusty green; pale but not cadaverous, with chalkstones in his hands. He said, that if it were not for the gout, his blindness would be tolerable.*

In the intervals of his pain, being made unable to use the common exercises, he used to swing in a chair, and sometimes played upon an organ.

He was now confessedly and visibly employed upon his poem, of which the progress might be noted by those with whom he was familiar; for he was obliged when he had
30 composed as many lines as his memory would conveniently retain, to employ some friend in writing them, having, at least for part of the time, no regular attendant. This gave opportunity to observations and reports.

Mr. Philips observes, that there was a very remarkable circumstance in the composure of " Paradise Lost," " which

I have a particular reason," says he, "to remember; for whereas I had the perusal of it from the very beginning, for some years, as I went from time to time to visit him, in parcels of ten, twenty, or thirty verses at a time (which, being written by whatever hand came next, might possibly want correction as to the orthography and pointing), having, as the summer came on, not been shewed any for a considerable while, and desiring the reason thereof, was answered, that his vein never happily flowed but from the Autumnal Equinox to the Vernal; and that whatever he 10 attempted at other times was never to his satisfaction, though he courted his fancy never so much; so that, in all the years he was about this poem, he may be said to have spent half his time therein."

Upon this relation Toland remarks, that in his opinion Philips has mistaken the time of the year; for Milton, in his Elegies, declares that with the advance of the Spring he feels the increase of his poetical force, *redeunt in carmina vires*. To this it is answered, that Philips could hardly mistake time so well marked; and it may be added, 20 that Milton might find different times of the year favourable to different parts of life. Mr. Richardson conceives it impossible that *such a work should be suspended for six months, or for one. It may go on faster or slower, but it must go on.* By what necessity it must continually go on, or why it might not be laid aside and resumed, it is not easy to discover.

This dependance of the soul upon the seasons, those temporary and periodical ebbs and flows of intellect, may, I suppose, justly be derided as the fumes of vain imagina- 30 tion. *Sapiens dominabitur astris.* The author that thinks himself weather-bound will find, with a little help from hellebore, that he is only idle or exhausted. But while this notion has possession of the head, it produces the inability which it supposes. Our powers owe much of their energy to our hopes; *possunt quia posse videntur.* When success seems attainable, diligence is enforced; but when it is admitted that the faculties are suppressed by a cross wind, or a cloudy sky, the day is given up without resistance; for who can contend with the course of Nature?

From such prepossessions Milton seems not to have been free. There prevailed in his time an opinion that the world was in its decay, and that we have had the misfor-
10 tune to be produced in the decrepitude of Nature. It was suspected that the whole creation languished, that neither trees nor animals had the height or bulk of their predecessors, and that every thing was daily sinking by gradual diminution. Milton appears to suspect that souls partake of the general degeneracy, and is not without some fear that his book is to be written in *an age too late* for heroick poesy.

Another opinion wanders about the world, and sometimes finds reception among wise men; an opinion that
20 restrains the operations of the mind to particular regions, and supposes that a luckless mortal may be born in a degree of latitude too high or too low for wisdom or for wit. From this fancy, wild as it is, he had not wholly cleared his head, when he feared lest the *climate* of his country might be *too cold* for flights of imagination.

Into a mind already occupied by such fancies, another not more reasonable might easily find its way. He that could fear lest his genius had fallen upon too old a world, or too chill a climate, might consistently magnify to him-
30 self the influence of the seasons, and believe his faculties to be vigorous only half the year.

His submission to the seasons was at least more reasonable than his dread of decaying Nature, or a frigid zone; for general causes must operate uniformly in a general abatement of mental power; if less could be performed by

the writer, less likewise would content the judges of his
work. Among this lagging race of frosty grovellers he
might still have risen into eminence by producing something which *they should not willingly let die.* However inferior to the heroes who were born in better ages, he might
still be great among his contemporaries, with the hope of
growing every day greater in the dwindle of posterity. He
might still be the giant of the pygmies, the one-eyed
monarch of the blind.

Of his artifices of study, or particular hours of composi- 10
tion, we have little account, and there was perhaps little
to be told. Richardson, who seems to have been very
diligent in his enquiries, but discovers always a wish to
find Milton discriminated from other men, relates, that
" he would sometimes lie awake whole nights, but not a
verse could he make; and on a sudden his poetical faculty
would rush upon him with an *impetus* or *œstrum,* and his
daughter was immediately called to secure what came. At
other times he would dictate perhaps forty lines in a
breath, and then reduce them to half the number." 20

These bursts of lights, and involutions of darkness;
these transient and involuntary excursions and retrocessions
of invention, having some appearance of deviation from
the common train of Nature, are eagerly caught by the
lovers of a wonder. Yet something of this inequality
happens to every man in every mode of exertion, manual
or mental. The mechanick cannot handle his hammer and
his file at all times with equal dexterity; there are hours,
he knows not why, when *his hand is out.* By Mr. Richardson's relation, casually conveyed, much regard cannot be 30
claimed. That, in his intellectual hour, Milton called for
his daughter *to secure what came,* may be questioned; for
unluckily it happens to be known that his daughters were
never taught to write; nor would he have been obliged, as
is universally confessed, to have employed any casual

visiter in disburthening his memory, if his daughter could
have performed the office.

The story of reducing his exuberance has been told of
other authors, and, though doubtless true of every fertile
and copious mind, seems to have been gratuitously trans-
ferred to Milton.

What he has told us, and we cannot now know more, is,
that he composed much of his poem in the night and morning, I suppose before his mind was disturbed with common
10 business; and that he poured out with great fluency his
unpremeditated verse. Versification, free, like his, from
the distresses of rhyme, must, by a work so long, be made
prompt and habitual; and, when his thoughts were once
adjusted, the words would come at his command.

At what particular times of his life the parts of his
work were written, cannot often be known. The beginning
of the third book shews that he had lost his sight; and
the Introduction to the seventh, that the return of the
King had clouded him with discountenance; and that he
20 was offended by the licentious festivity of the Restoration.
There are no other internal notes of time. Milton, being
now cleared from all effects of his disloyalty, had nothing
required from him but the common duty of living in quiet,
to be rewarded with the common right of protection: but
this, which, when he sculked from the approach of his
King, was perhaps more than he hoped, seems not to have
satisfied him; for no sooner is he safe, than he finds himself in danger, *fallen on evil days and evil tongues, and with
darkness and with danger compass'd round.* This darkness,
30 had his eyes been better employed, had undoubtedly de-
served compassion : but to add the mention of danger was
ungrateful and unjust. He was fallen indeed on *evil days ;*
the time was come in which regicides could no longer
boast their wickedness. But of *evil tongues* for Milton to
complain, required impudence at least equal to his other

powers; Milton, whose warmest advocates must allow, that
he never spared any asperity of reproach or brutality of
insolence.

But the charge itself seems to be false; for it would be
hard to recollect any reproach cast upon him, either serious
or ludicrous, through the whole remaining part of his life.
He pursued his studies, or his amusements, without perse-
cution, molestation, or insult. Such is the reverence paid
to great abilities, however misused: they who contemplated
in Milton the scholar and the wit, were contented to forget 10
the reviler of his King.

When the plague (1665) raged in London, Milton took
refuge at Chalfont in Bucks; where Elwood, who had
taken the house for him, first saw a complete copy of
"Paradise Lost," and, having perused it, said to him,
"Thou hast said a great deal upon 'Paradise Lost;' what
hast thou to say upon 'Paradise Found?'"

Next year, when the danger of infection had ceased, he
returned to Bunhill-fields, and designed the publication of
his poem. A license was necessary, and he could expect 20
no great kindness from a chaplain of the archbishop of
Canterbury. He seems, however, to have been treated with
tenderness; for though objections were made to particular
passages, and among them to the simile of the sun eclipsed
in the first book, yet the license was granted; and he sold
his copy, April 27, 1667, to Samuel Simmons, for an immediate payment of five pounds, with a stipulation to
receive five pounds more when thirteen hundred should be
sold of the first edition: and again, five pounds after the
sale of the same number of the second edition: and another 30
five pounds after the same sale of the third. None of the
three editions were to be extended beyond fifteen hundred
copies.

The first edition was ten books, in a small quarto. The
titles were varied from year to year; and an advertisement

and the arguments of the books were omitted in some copies, and inserted in others.

The sale gave him in two years a right to his second payment, for which the receipt was signed April 26, 1669. The second edition was not given till 1674; it was printed in small octavo; and the number of books was increased to twelve, by a division of the seventh and twelfth; and some other small improvements were made. The third edition was published in 1678; and the widow, to whom 10 the copy was then to devolve, sold all her claims to Simmons for eight pounds, according to her receipt given Dec. 21, 1680. Simmons had already agreed to transfer the whole right to Brabazon Aylmer for twenty-five pounds; and Aylmer sold to Jacob Tonson half, August 17, 1683, and half, March 24, 1690, at a price considerably enlarged. In the history of "Paradise Lost," a deduction thus minute will rather gratify than fatigue.

The slow sale and tardy reputation of this poem have been always mentioned as evidences of neglected merit, and 20 of the uncertainty of literary fame; and enquiries have been made, and conjectures offered, about the causes of its long obscurity and late reception. But has the case been truly stated? Have not lamentation and wonder been lavished on an evil that was never felt?

That in the reigns of Charles and James the "Paradise Lost" received no publick acclamations, is readily confessed. Wit and literature were on the side of the Court: and who that solicited favour or fashion would venture to praise the defender of the regicides? All that he himself could think 30 his due, from *evil tongues* in *evil days*, was that reverential silence which was generously preserved. But it cannot be inferred that his poem was not read, or not, however unwillingly, admired.

The sale, if it be considered, will justify the publick. Those who have no power to judge of past times but by their own, should always doubt their conclusions. The call for books was not in Milton's age what it is in the present. To read was not then a general amusement; neither traders, nor often gentlemen, thought themselves disgraced by ignorance. The women had not then aspired to literature, nor was every house supplied with a closet of knowledge. Those, indeed, who professed learning, were not less learned than at any other time; but of that middle race of students who read for pleasure or accomplishment, and who buy the numerous products of modern typography, the number was then comparatively small. To prove the paucity of readers, it may be sufficient to remark, that the nation had been satisfied, from 1623 to 1664, that is, forty-one years, with only two editions of the works of Shakspeare, which probably did not together make one thousand copies.

The sale of thirteen hundred copies in two years, in opposition to so much recent enmity, and to a style of versification new to all and disgusting to many, was an uncommon example of the prevalence of genius. The demand did not immediately increase; for many more readers than were supplied at first the nation did not afford. Only three thousand were sold in eleven years; for it forced its way without assistance: its admirers did not dare to publish their opinion; and the opportunities now given of attracting notice by advertisements were then very few; the means of proclaiming the publication of new books have been produced by that general literature which now pervades the nation through all its ranks.

But the reputation and price of the copy still advanced, till the Revolution put an end to the secrecy of love, and "Paradise Lost" broke into open view with sufficient security of kind reception.

Fancy can hardly forbear to conjecture with what temper Milton surveyed the silent progress of his work, and marked his reputation stealing its way in a kind of subterraneous current through fear and silence. I cannot but conceive him calm and confident, little disappointed, not at all dejected, relying on his own merit with steady consciousness, and waiting, without impatience, the vicissitudes of opinion, and the impartiality of a future generation.

In the mean time he continued his studies, and supplied the want of sight by a very odd expedient, of which Philips gives the following account:

10　　Mr. Philips tells us, "that though our author had daily about him one or other to read, some persons of man's estate, who, of their own accord, greedily catched at the opportunity of being his readers, that they might as well reap the benefit of what they read to him, as oblige him by the benefit of their reading; and others of younger years were sent by their parents to the same end: yet excusing only the eldest daughter, by reason of her bodily infirmity, and difficult utterance of speech (which, to say truth, I doubt was the principal cause of excusing her), the other 20 two were condemned to the performance of reading, and exactly pronouncing of all the languages of whatever book he should, at one time or other, think fit to peruse, viz. the Hebrew (and I think the Syriac), the Greek, the Latin, the Italian, Spanish, and French. All which sorts of books to be confined to read, without understanding one word, must needs be a trial of patience almost beyond endurance. Yet it was endured by both for a long time, though the irksomeness of this employment could not be always concealed, but broke out more and more into expressions of uneasiness; 30 so that at length they were all, even the eldest also, sent out to learn some curious and ingenious sorts of manufacture, that are proper for women to learn; particularly embroideries in gold or silver."

In the scene of misery which this mode of intellectual labour sets before our eyes, it is hard to determine whether the daughters or the father are most to be lamented. A language not understood can never be so read as to give pleasure, and very seldom so as to convey meaning. If few men would have had resolution to write books with such embarrassments, few likewise would have wanted ability to find some better expedient.

Three years after his "Paradise Lost" (1667), he published his "History of England," comprising the whole fable of Geoffry of Monmouth, and continued to the Norman invasion. Why he should have given the first part, which he seems not to believe, and which is universally rejected, it is difficult to conjecture. The style is harsh; but it has something of rough vigour, which perhaps may often strike, though it cannot please.

On this history the licenser again fixed his claws, and before he would transmit it to the press tore out several parts. Some censures of the Saxon monks were taken away, lest they should be applied to the modern clergy; and a character of the Long Parliament, and Assembly of Divines, was excluded; of which the author gave a copy to the earl of Anglesea, and which, being afterwards published, has since been inserted in its proper place.

The same year were printed "Paradise Regained," and "Samson Agonistes," a tragedy written in imitation of the Ancients, and never designed by the author for the stage. As these poems were published by another bookseller, it has been asked, whether Simmons was discouraged from receiving them by the slow sale of the former. Why a writer changed his bookseller a hundred years ago, I am far from hoping to discover. Certainly, he who in two years sells thirteen hundred copies of a volume in quarto, bought for two payments of five pounds each, has no reason to repent his purchase.

When Milton shewed "Paradise Regained" to Elwood, "This," said he, "is owing to you; for you put it in my

head by the question you put to me at Chalfont, which
otherwise I had not thought of."

His last poetical offspring was his favourite. He could
not, as Elwood relates, endure to hear "Paradise Lost"
preferred to "Paradise Regained." Many causes may
vitiate a writer's judgement of his own works. On that
which has cost him much labour he sets a high value, because he is unwilling to think that he has been diligent in
vain; what has been produced without toilsome efforts is
10 considered with delight, as a proof of vigorous faculties
and fertile invention; and the last work, whatever it be,
has necessarily most of the grace of novelty. Milton,
however it happened, had this prejudice, and had it to
himself.

To that multiplicity of attainments, and extent of com-
prehension, that entitle this great author to our veneration,
may be added a kind of humble dignity, which did not
disdain the meanest services to literature. The epic poet,
the controvertist, the politician, having already descended
20 to accommodate children with a book of rudiments, now,
in the last years of his life, composed a book of Logick,
for the initiation of students in philosophy: and published
(1672) "Artis Logicæ plenior Institutio ad Petri Rami
methodum concinnata;" that is, "A new Scheme of Logick, according to the Method of Ramus." I know not
whether, even in this book, he did not intend an act of
hostility against the Universities; for Ramus was one of
the first oppugners of the old philosophy, who disturbed
with innovations the quiet of the schools.

30 His polemical disposition again revived. He had now
been safe so long, that he forgot his fears, and published a
"Treatise of true Religion, Heresy, Schism, Toleration, and
the best Means to prevent the Growth of Popery."

But this little tract is modestly written, with respectful
mention of the Church of England, and an appeal to the

thirty-nine articles. His principle of toleration is, agreement in the sufficiency of the Scriptures; and he extends it to all who, whatever their opinions are, profess to derive them from the sacred books. The papists appeal to other testimonies, and are therefore in his opinion not to be permitted the liberty of either publick or private worship; for though they plead conscience, *we have no warrant,* he says, *to regard conscience which is not grounded in Scripture.*

Those who are not convinced by his reasons, may be perhaps delighted with his wit. The term *Roman catholick* is, he says, *one of the Pope's bulls; it is particular universal,* or *catholick schismatick.*

He has, however, something better. As the best preservative against Popery, he recommends the diligent perusal of the Scriptures; a duty, from which he warns the busy part of mankind not to think themselves excused.

He now reprinted his juvenile poems, with some additions.

In the last year of his life he sent to the press, seeming to take delight in publication, a collection of Familiar Epistles in Latin; to which, being too few to make a volume, he added some academical exercises, which perhaps he perused with pleasure, as they recalled to his memory the days of youth; but for which nothing but veneration for his name could now procure a reader.

When he had attained his sixty-sixth year, the gout, with which he had been long tormented, prevailed over the enfeebled powers of nature. He died by a quiet and silent expiration, about the tenth of November 1674, at his house in Bunhill-fields; and was buried next his father in the chancel of St. Giles at Cripplegate. His funeral was very splendidly and numerously attended.

Upon his grave there is supposed to have been no memorial; but in our time a monument has been erected

in Westminster-Abbey *To the Author of Paradise Lost*, by
Mr. Benson, who has in the inscription bestowed more
words upon himself than upon Milton.

When the inscription for the monument of Philips, in
which he was said to be *soli Miltono secundus*, was exhibited to Dr. Sprat, then dean of Westminster, he refused
to admit it; the name of Milton was, in his opinion, too
detestable to be read on the wall of a building dedicated
to devotion. Atterbury, who succeeded him, being author
10 of the inscription, permitted its reception. "And such
has been the change of publick opinion," said Dr. Gregory,
from whom I heard this account, "that I have seen erected
in the church a statue of that man, whose name I once
knew considered as a pollution of its walls."

Milton has the reputation of having been in his youth
eminently beautiful, so as to have been called the Lady of
his college. His hair, which was of a light brown, parted at
the foretop, and hung down upon his shoulders, according
to the picture which he has given of Adam. He was,
20 however, not of the heroick stature, but rather below the
middle size, according to Mr. Richardson, who mentions
him as having narrowly escaped from being *short and thick*.
He was vigorous and active, and delighted in the exercise
of the sword, in which he is related to have been eminently
skilful. His weapon was, I believe, not the rapier, but the
backsword, of which he recommends the use in his book on
Education.

His eyes are said never to have been bright; but, if he
was a dexterous fencer, they must have been once quick.

30 His domestick habits, so far as they are known, were
those of a severe student. He drank little strong drink of
any kind, and fed without excess in quantity, and in his
earlier years without delicacy of choice. In his youth he
studied late at night; but afterwards changed his hours,
and rested in bed from nine to four in the summer, and

five in winter. The course of his day was best known after he was blind. When he first rose, he heard a chapter in the Hebrew Bible, and then studied till twelve ; then took some exercise for an hour ; then dined ; then played on the organ, and sung, or heard another sing ; then studied to six ; then entertained his visiters till eight ; then supped, and, after a pipe of tobacco and a glass of water, went to bed.

So is his life described ; but this even tenour appears attainable only in Colleges. He that lives in the world 10 will sometimes have the succession of his practice broken and confused. Visiters, of whom Milton is represented to have had great numbers, will come and stay unseasonably ; business, of which every man has some, must be done when others will do it.

When he did not care to rise early, he had something read to him by his bedside ; perhaps at this time his daughters were employed. He composed much in the morning, and dictated in the day, sitting obliquely in an elbow-chair, with his leg thrown over the arm. 20

Fortune appears not to have had much of his care. In the civil wars he lent his personal estate to the parliament ; but when, after the contest was decided, he solicited repayment, he met not only with neglect, but *sharp rebuke ;* and, having tired both himself and his friends, was given up to poverty and hopeless indignation, till he shewed how able he was to do greater service. He was then made Latin secretary, with two hundred pounds a year; and had a thousand pounds for his " Defence of the People." His widow, who, after his death, retired to Namptwich in 30 Cheshire, and died about 1729, is said to have reported that he lost two thousand pounds by entrusting it to a scrivener; and that, in the general depredation upon the Church, he had grasped an estate of about sixty pounds a year belonging to Westminster Abbey, which, like other

E

sharers of the plunder of rebellion, he was afterwards
obliged to return. Two thousand pounds, which he had
placed in the Excise-office, were also lost. There is yet no
reason to believe that he was ever reduced to indigence.
His wants, being few, were competently supplied. He
sold his library before his death, and left his family fifteen
hundred pounds, on which his widow laid hold, and only
gave one hundred to each of his daughters.

His literature was unquestionably great. He read all
10 the languages which are considered either as learned or
polite; Hebrew, with its two dialects, Greek, Latin, Italian,
French, and Spanish. In Latin his skill was such as places
him in the first rank of writers and criticks; and he appears to have cultivated Italian with uncommon diligence.
The books in which his daughter, who used to read to him,
represented him as most delighting, after Homer, which he
could almost repeat, were Ovid's "Metamorphoses" and
Euripides. His Euripides is, by Mr. Cradock's kindness,
now in my hands: the margin is sometimes noted; but
20 I have found nothing remarkable.

Of the English poets he set most value upon Spenser,
Shakspeare, and Cowley. Spenser was apparently his
favourite: Shakspeare he may easily be supposed to like,
with every other skilful reader; but I should not have
expected that Cowley, whose ideas of excellence were different from his own, would have had much of his approbation. His character of Dryden, who sometimes visited him,
was, that he was a good rhymist, but no poet.

His theological opinions are said to have been first
30 Calvinistical; and afterwards, perhaps when he began to
hate the Presbyterians, to have extended towards Arminianism. In the mixed questions of theology and government, he never thinks that he can recede far enough
from popery, or prelacy; but what Baudius says of Erasmus seems applicable to him, *magis habuit quod fugeret,*

quam quod sequeretur. He had determined rather what to condemn, than what to approve. He has not associated himself with any denomination of Protestants : we know rather what he was not, than what he was. He was not of the church of Rome; he was not of the church of England.

To be of no church, is dangerous. Religion, of which the rewards are distant, and which is animated only by Faith and Hope, will glide by degrees out of the mind, unless it be invigorated and reimpressed by external ordi- 10 nances, by stated calls to worship, and the salutary influence of example. Milton, who appears to have had full conviction of the truth of Christianity, and to have regarded the Holy Scriptures with the profoundest veneration, to have been untainted by any heretical peculiarity of opinion, and to have lived in a confirmed belief of the immediate and occasional agency of Providence, yet grew old without any visible worship. In the distribution of his hours, there was no hour of prayer, either solitary, or with his household ; omitting publick prayers, he omitted 20 all.

Of this omission the reason has been sought, upon a supposition which ought never to be made, that men live with their own approbation, and justify their conduct to themselves. Prayer certainly was not thought superfluous by him, who represents our first parents as praying acceptably in the state of innocence, and efficaciously after their fall. That he lived without prayer can hardly be affirmed; his studies and meditations were an habitual prayer. The neglect of it in his family was probably a 30 fault for which he condemned himself, and which he intended to correct, but that death, as too often happens, intercepted his reformation.

His political notions were those of an acrimonious and surly republican, for which it is not known that he gave any better reason than that *a popular government was the most frugal; for the trappings of a monarchy would set up an ordinary commonwealth.* It is surely very shallow policy, that supposes money to be the chief good; and even this, without considering that the support and expence of a Court is, for the most part, only a particular kind of traffick, by which money is circulated, without any national impoverishment.

Milton's republicanism was, I am afraid, founded in an envious hatred of greatness, and a sullen desire of independence; in petulance impatient of controul, and pride disdainful of superiority. He hated monarchs in the state, and prelates in the church; for he hated all whom he was required to obey. It is to be suspected, that his predominant desire was to destroy rather than establish, and that he felt not so much the love of liberty as repugnance to authority.

It has been observed, that they who most loudly clamour for liberty do not most liberally grant it. What we know of Milton's character, in domestick relations, is, that he was severe and arbitrary. His family consisted of women; and there appears in his books something like a Turkish contempt of females, as subordinate and inferior beings. That his own daughters might not break the ranks, he suffered them to be depressed by a mean and penurious education. He thought women made only for obedience, and man only for rebellion.

Of his family some account may be expected. His sister, first married to Mr. Philips, afterwards married Mr. Agar, a friend of her first husband, who succeeded him in the Crown-office. She had by her first husband Edward and John, the two nephews whom Milton educated; and by her second, two daughters.

His brother, Sir Christopher, had two daughters, Mary and Catherine, and a son Thomas, who succeeded Agar in the Crown-office, and left a daughter living in 1749 in Grosvenor-street.

Milton had children only by his first wife; Anne, Mary, and Deborah. Anne, though deformed, married a master-builder, and died of her first child. Mary died single. Deborah married Abraham Clark, a weaver in Spitalfields, and lived seventy-six years, to August, 1727. This is the daughter of whom public mention has been made. She could repeat the first lines of Homer, the "Metamorphoses," and some of Euripides, by having often read them. Yet 10 here incredulity is ready to make a stand. Many repetitions are necessary to fix in the memory lines not understood; and why should Milton wish or want to hear them so often! These lines were at the beginning of the poems. Of a book written in a language not understood, the beginning raises no more attention than the end; and as those that understand it know commonly the beginning best, its rehearsal will seldom be necessary. It is not likely that Milton required any passage to be so much repeated as that his daughter could learn it; nor likely 20 that he desired the initial lines to be read at all: nor that the daughter, weary of the drudgery of pronouncing unideal sounds, would voluntarily commit them to memory.

To this gentlewoman Addison made a present, and promised some establishment; but died soon after. Queen Caroline sent her fifty guineas. She had seven sons and three daughters; but none of them had any children, except her son Caleb and her daughter Elizabeth. Caleb went to Fort St. George in the East Indies, and had two 30 sons, of whom nothing is now known. Elizabeth married Thomas Foster, a weaver in Spitalfields, and had seven children, who all died. She kept a petty grocer's or chandler's shop, first at Holloway, and afterwards in Cock-lane near Shoreditch Church. She knew little of her

grandfather, and that little was not good. She told of his
harshness to his daughters, and his refusal to have them
taught to write; and, in opposition to other accounts,
represented him as delicate, though temperate, in his diet.

In 1750, April 5, " Comus " was played for her benefit.
She had so little acquaintance with diversion or gaiety,
that she did not know what was intended when a benefit
was offered her. The profits of the night were only one
hundred and thirty pounds, though Dr. Newton brought a
10 large contribution; and twenty pounds were given by
Tonson, a man who is to be praised as often as he is
named. Of this sum one hundred pounds was placed in
the stocks, after some debate between her and her husband
in whose name it should be entered; and the rest aug-
mented their little stock, with which they removed to
Islington. This was the greatest benefaction that " Paradise Lost " ever procured the author's descendents; and
to this he who has now attempted to relate his Life, had the
honour of contributing a Prologue.

20   In the examination of Milton's poetical works, I shall
pay so much regard to time as to begin with his juvenile
productions. For his early pieces he seems to have had a
degree of fondness not very laudable: what he has once
written he resolves to preserve, and gives to the publick
an unfinished poem, which he broke off because he was
nothing satisfied with what he had done, supposing his
readers less nice than himself. These preludes to his
future labours are in Italian, Latin, and English. Of the
Italian I cannot pretend to speak as a critick; but I
30 have heard them commended by a man well qualified to
decide their merit. The Latin pieces are lusciously elegant;
but the delight which they afford is rather by the exquisite
imitation of the ancient writers, by the purity of the
diction, and the harmony of the numbers, than by any

power of invention, or vigour of sentiment. They are not all of equal value; the elegies excell the odes; and some of the exercises on Gunpowder Treason might have been spared.

The English poems, though they make no promises of "Paradise Lost," have this evidence of genius, that they have a cast original and unborrowed. But their peculiarity is not excellence: if they differ from verses of others, they differ for the worse; for they are too often distinguished by repulsive harshness; the combinations of words are new, 10 but they are not pleasing; the rhymes and epithets seem to be laboriously sought, and violently applied.

That in the early parts of his life he wrote with much care appears from his manuscripts, happily preserved at Cambridge, in which many of his smaller works are found as they were first written, with the subsequent corrections. Such reliques shew how excellence is acquired; what we hope ever to do with ease, we may learn first to do with diligence.

Those who admire the beauties of this great poet, some- 20 times force their own judgment into false approbation of his little pieces, and prevail upon themselves to think that admirable which is only singular. All that short composi-tions can commonly attain is neatness and elegance. Milton never learned the art of doing little things with grace; he overlooked the milder excellence of suavity and softness; he was a *Lion* that had no skill *in dandling the Kid.*

One of the poems on which much praise has been be-stowed is "Lycidas;" of which the diction is harsh, the 30 rhymes uncertain, and the numbers unpleasing. What beauty there is, we must therefore seek in the sentiments and images. It is not to be considered as the effusion of real passion; for passion runs not after remote allusions and obscure opinions. Passion plucks no berries from the

myrtle and ivy, nor calls upon Arethuse and Mincius, nor
tells of rough *satyrs* and *fauns with cloven heel.* Where
there is leisure for fiction there is little grief.

In this poem there is no nature, for there is no truth ;
there is no art, for there is nothing new.   Its form is that
of a pastoral, easy, vulgar, and therefore disgusting : whatever images it can supply, are long ago exhausted ; and
its inherent improbability always forces dissatisfaction on
the mind.   When Cowley tells of Hervey that they
10 studied together, it is easy to suppose how much he must
miss the companion of his labours, and the partner of his
discoveries ; but what image of tenderness can be excited
by these lines !

> We drove a-field, and both together heard
> What time the grey fly winds her sultry horn,
> Battening our flocks with the fresh dews of night.

We know that they never drove a field, and that they had
no flocks to batten ; and though it be allowed that the
representation may be allegorical, the true meaning is so
20 uncertain and remote, that it is never sought because it
cannot be known when it is found.

Among the flocks, and copses, and flowers, appear the
heathen deities ; Jove and Phœbus, Neptune and Æolus,
with a long train of mythological imagery, such as a
College easily supplies.   Nothing can less display knowledge, or less exercise invention, than to tell how a shepherd has lost his companion, and must now feed his flocks
alone, without any judge of his skill in piping ; and how
one god asks another god what is become of Lycidas,
30 and how neither god can tell.   He who thus grieves will
excite no sympathy ; he who thus praises will confer no
honour.

This poem has yet a grosser fault.   With these trifling
fictions are mingled the most awful and sacred truths,

such as ought never to be polluted with such irreverend combinations. The shepherd likewise is now a feeder of sheep, and afterwards an ecclesiastical pastor, a super-intendent of a Christian flock. Such equivocations are always unskilful; but here they are indecent, and at least approach to impiety, of which, however, I believe the writer not to have been conscious.

Such is the power of reputation justly acquired, that its blaze drives away the eye from nice examination. Surely no man could have fancied that he read "Lycidas" with pleasure, had he not known its author.

Of the two pieces, "L'Allegro" and "Il Penseroso," I believe opinion is uniform; every man that reads them, reads them with pleasure. The author's design is not, what Theobald has remarked, merely to shew how objects derive their colours from the mind, by representing the operation of the same things upon the gay and the melan-choly temper, or upon the same man as he is differently disposed; but rather how, among the successive variety of appearances, every disposition of mind takes hold on those by which it may be gratified.

The *chearful* man hears the lark in the morning; the *pensive* man hears the nightingale in the evening. The *chearful* man sees the cock strut, and hears the horn and hounds echo in the wood; then walks *not unseen* to ob-serve the glory of the rising sun, or listen to the singing milk-maid, and view the labours of the plowman and the mower; then casts his eyes about him over scenes of smiling plenty, and looks up to the distant tower, the residence of some fair inhabitant; thus he pursues rural gaiety through a day of labour or of play, and delights himself at night with the fanciful narratives of super-stitious ignorance.

The *pensive* man, at one time, walks *unseen* to muse at midnight; and at another hears the sullen curfew. If the

weather drives him home, he sits in a room lighted only by
glowing embers; or by a lonely lamp outwatches the North
Star, to discover the habitation of separate souls, and varies
the shades of meditation, by contemplating the magnificent
or pathetick scenes of tragick and epic poetry. When the
morning comes, a morning gloomy with rain and wind, he
walks into the dark trackless woods, falls asleep by some
murmuring water, and with melancholy enthusiasm expects
some dream of prognostication, or some musick played by
10 aerial performers.

Both Mirth and Melancholy are solitary, silent inhabitants of the breast that neither receive nor transmit communication; no mention is therefore made of a philosophical friend, or a pleasant companion. The seriousness
does not arise from any participation of calamity, nor the
gaiety from the pleasures of the bottle.

The man of *chearfulness,* having exhausted the country,
tries what *towered cities* will afford, and mingles with scenes
of splendor, gay assemblies, and nuptial festivities; but he
20 mingles a mere spectator, as, when the learned comedies of
Jonson, or the wild dramas of Shakspeare, are exhibited,
he attends the theatre.

The *pensive* man never loses himself in crowds, but
walks the cloister, or frequents the cathedral. Milton
probably had not yet forsaken the Church.

Both his characters delight in musick; but he seems to
think that chearful notes would have obtained from Pluto
a compleat dismission of Eurydice, of whom solemn sounds
only procured a conditional release.

30 For the old age of Chearfulness he makes no provision;
but Melancholy he conducts with great dignity to the close
of life. His Chearfulness is without levity, and his Pensiveness without asperity.

Through these two poems the images are properly
selected, and nicely distinguished; but the colours of the

diction seem not sufficiently discriminated. I know not
whether the characters are kept sufficiently apart. No
mirth can, indeed, be found in his melancholy; but I am
afraid that I always meet some melancholy in his mirth.
They are two noble efforts of imagination.

The greatest of his juvenile performances is the " Mask
of Comus ;" in which may very plainly be discovered the
dawn or twilight of " Paradise Lost." Milton appears to
have formed very early that system of diction, and mode of
verse, which his maturer judgement approved, and from 10
which he never endeavoured nor desired to deviate.

Nor does " Comus " afford only a specimen of his language; it exhibits likewise his power of description and
his vigour of sentiment, employed in the praise and defence
of virtue. A work more truly poetical is rarely found;
allusions, images, and descriptive epithets, embellish
almost every period with lavish decoration. As a series
of lines, therefore, it may be considered as worthy of all
the admiration with which the votaries have received it.

As a drama it is deficient. The action is not probable. 20
A Masque, in those parts where supernatural intervention
is admitted, must indeed be given up to all the freaks of
imagination; but, so far as the action is merely human, it
ought to be reasonable, which can hardly be said of the
conduct of the two brothers ; who, when their sister sinks
with fatigue in a pathless wilderness, wander both away
together in search of berries too far to find their way back,
and leave a helpless Lady to all the sadness and danger of
solitude. This however is a defect overbalanced by its
convenience. 30

What deserves more reprehension is, that the prologue
spoken in the wild wood by the attendant Spirit is addressed
to the audience; a mode of communication so contrary to
nature of dramatick representation, that no precedents can
support it.

The discourse of the Spirit is too long; an objection that may be made to almost all the following speeches : they have not the spriteliness of a dialogue animated by reciprocal contention, but seem rather declamations deliberately composed, and formally repeated, on a moral question. The auditor therefore listens as to a lecture, without passion, without anxiety.

The song of Comus has airiness and jollity; but, what may recommend Milton's morals as well as his poetry, the 10 invitations to pleasure are so general, that they excite no distinct images of corrupt enjoyment, and take no dangerous hold on the fancy.

The following soliloquies of Comus and the Lady are elegant, but tedious. The song must owe much to the voice, if it ever can delight. At last the Brothers enter, with too much tranquillity; and when they have feared lest their sister should be in danger, and hoped that she is not in danger, the Elder makes a speech in praise of chastity, and the Younger finds how fine it is to be a 20 philosopher.

Then descends the Spirit in form of a shepherd; and the Brother, instead of being in haste to ask his help, praises his singing, and enquires his business in that place. It is remarkable, that at this interview the Brother is taken with a short fit of rhyming. The Spirit relates that the Lady is in the power of Comus; the Brother moralises again; and the Spirit makes a long narration, of no use because it is false, and therefore unsuitable to a good Being.

In all these parts the language is poetical, and the senti-
30 ments are generous; but there is something wanting to allure attention.

The dispute between the Lady and Comus is the most animated and affecting scene of the drama, and wants nothing but a brisker reciprocation of objections and replies, to invite attention, and detain it.

The songs are vigorous, and full of imagery; but they are harsh in their diction, and not very musical in their numbers.

Throughout the whole, the figures are too bold, and the language too luxuriant for dialogue. It is a drama in the epic style, inelegantly splendid, and tediously instructive.

The " Sonnets " were written in different parts of Milton's life, upon different occasions. They deserve not any particular criticism; for of the best it can only be said, that they are not bad; and perhaps only the eighth and the 10 twenty-first are truly entitled to this slender commendation. The fabrick of a sonnet, however adapted to the Italian language, has never succeeded in ours, which, having greater variety of termination, requires the rhymes to be often changed.

Those little pieces may be dispatched without much anxiety; a greater work calls for greater care. I am now to examine "Paradise Lost;" a poem, which, considered with respect to design, may claim the first place, and with respect to performance the second, among the productions 20 of the human mind.

By the general consent of criticks, the first praise of genius is due to the writer of an epick poem, as it requires an assemblage of all the powers which are singly sufficient for other compositions. Poetry is the art of uniting pleasure with truth, by calling imagination to the help of reason. Epick poetry undertakes to teach the most important truths by the most pleasing precepts, and therefore relates some great event in the most affecting manner. History must supply the writer with the rudiments of 30 narration, which he must improve and exalt by a nobler art, must animate by dramatick energy, and diversify by retrospection and anticipation; morality must teach him the exact bounds, and different shades, of vice and virtue; from policy, and the practice of life, he has to learn the

discriminations of character, and the tendency of the
passions, either single or combined ; and physiology must
supply him with illustrations and images. To put these
materials to poetical use, is required an imagination capable
of painting nature, and realizing fiction. Nor is he yet a
poet till he has attained the whole extension of his language,
distinguished all the delicacies of phrase, and all the colours
of words, and learned to adjust their different sounds to all
the varieties of metrical modulation.

10   Bossu is of opinion that the poet's first work is to find
a *moral*, which his fable is afterwards to illustrate and
establish. This seems to have been the process only of
Milton ; the moral of other poems is incidental and conse-
quent ; in Milton's only it is essential and intrinsick. His
purpose was the most useful and the most arduous ; *to
vindicate the ways of God to man ;* to shew the reasonableness of religion, and the necessity of obedience to the
Divine Law.

To convey this moral, there must be a *fable*, a narration
20 artfully constructed, so as to excite curiosity, and surprise
expectation. In this part of his work, Milton must be confessed to have equalled every other poet. He has involved
in his account of the Fall of Man the events which preceded, and those that were to follow it : he has interwoven
the whole system of theology with such propriety, that
every part appears to be necessary ; and scarcely any recital
is wished shorter for the sake of quickening the progress
of the main action.

The subject of an epic poem is naturally an event of
30 great importance. That of Milton is not the destruction
of a city, the conduct of a colony, or the foundation of an
empire. His subject is the fate of worlds, the revolutions
of heaven and of earth ; rebellion against the Supreme
King, raised by the highest order of created beings ; the
overthrow of their host, and the punishment of their crime ;

the creation of a new race of reasonable creatures; their original happiness and innocence, their forfeiture of immortality, and their restoration to hope and peace.

Great events can be hastened or retarded only by persons of elevated dignity. Before the greatness displayed in Milton's poem, all other greatness shrinks away. The weakest of his agents are the highest and noblest of human beings, the original parents of mankind; with whose actions the elements consented; on whose rectitude, or deviation of will, depended the state of terrestrial nature, and the 10 condition of all the future inhabitants of the globe.

Of the other agents in the poem, the chief are such as it is irreverence to name on slight occasions. The rest were lower powers;

> "—of which the least could wield
> Those elements, and arm him with the force
> Of all their regions;"

powers, which only the controul of Omnipotence restrains from laying creation waste, and filling the vast expanse of space with ruin and confusion. To display the motives and 20 actions of beings thus superiour, so far as human reason can examine them, or human imagination represent them, is the task which this mighty poet has undertaken and performed.

In the examination of epick poems much speculation is commonly employed upon the *characters*. The characters in the "Paradise Lost," which admit of examination, are those of angels and of man; of angels good and evil; of man in his innocent and sinful state.

Among the angels, the virtue of Raphael is mild and 30 placid, of easy condescension and free communication; that of Michael is regal and lofty, and, as may seem, attentive to the dignity of his own nature. Abdiel and Gabriel appear occasionally, and act as every incident requires; the solitary fidelity of Abdiel is very amiably painted.

Of the evil angels the characters are more diversified. To Satan, as Addison observes, such sentiments are given as suit *the most exalted and most depraved being*. Milton has been censured, by Clarke, for the impiety which sometimes breaks from Satan's mouth. For there are thoughts, as he justly remarks, which no observation of character can justify, because no good man would willingly permit them to pass, however transiently, through his own mind. To make Satan speak as a rebel, without any such expres-
10 sions as might taint the reader's imagination, was indeed one of the great difficulties in Milton's undertaking, and I cannot but think that he has extricated himself with great happiness. There is in Satan's speeches little that can give pain to a pious ear. The language of rebellion cannot be the same with that of obedience. The malignity of Satan foams in haughtiness and obstinacy; but his expressions are commonly general, and no otherwise offensive than as they are wicked.

The other chiefs of the celestial rebellion are very
20 judiciously discriminated in the first and second books; and the ferocious character of Moloch appears, both in the battle and the council, with exact consistency.

To Adam and to Eve are given, during their innocence, such sentiments as innocence can generate and utter. Their love is pure benevolence and mutual veneration; their repasts are without luxury, and their diligence without toil. Their addresses to their Maker have little more than the voice of admiration and gratitude. Fruition left them nothing to ask, and Innocence left them nothing to
30 fear.

But with guilt enter distrust and discord, mutual accusation, and stubborn self-defence; they regard each other with alienated minds, and dread their Creator as the avenger of their transgression. At last they seek shelter in his mercy, soften to repentance, and melt in supplication.

Both before and after the Fall, the superiority of Adam is diligently sustained.

Of the *probable* and the *marvellous*, two parts of a vulgar epic poem, which immerge the critick in deep consideration, the "Paradise Lost" requires little to be said. It contains the history of a miracle, of Creation and Redemption; it displays the power and the mercy of the Supreme Being; the probable therefore is marvellous, and the marvellous is probable. The substance of the narrative is truth; and as truth allows no choice, it is, like necessity, superior to rule. 10 To the accidental or adventitious parts, as to every thing human, some slight exceptions may be made. But the main fabrick is immovably supported.

It is justly remarked by Addison, that this poem has, by the nature of its subject, the advantage above all others, that it is universally and perpetually interesting. All mankind will, through all ages, bear the same relation to Adam and to Eve, and must partake of that good and evil which extend to themselves. *deus ex machina*

Of the *machinery*, so called from Θεὸς ἀπὸ μηχανῆς, by 20 which is meant the occasional interposition of supernatural power, another fertile topic of critical remarks, here is no room to speak, because every thing is done under the immediate and visible direction of Heaven; but the rule is so far observed, that no part of the action could have been accomplished by any other means.

Of *episodes*, I think there are only two, contained in Raphael's relation of the war in heaven, and Michael's prophetick account of the changes to happen in this world. Both are closely connected with the great action; one 30 was necessary to Adam as a warning, the other as a consolation.

To the compleatness or *integrity* of the design nothing can be objected; it has distinctly and clearly what Aristotle requires, a beginning, a middle, and an end. There is

F

perhaps no poem, of the same length, from which so little
can be taken without apparent mutilation. Here are no
funeral games, nor is there any long description of a shield.
The short digressions at the beginning of the third, seventh,
and ninth books, might doubtless be spared; but super-
fluities so beautiful, who would take away? or who does
not wish that the author of the "Iliad" had gratified suc-
ceeding ages with a little knowledge of himself? Perhaps
no passages are more frequently or more attentively read
10 than those extrinsick paragraphs; and, since the end of
poetry is pleasure, that cannot be unpoetical with which
all are pleased.

The questions, whether the action of the poem be
strictly *one*, whether the poem can be properly termed
heroick, and who is the hero, are raised by such readers as
draw their principles of judgement rather from books
than from reason. Milton, though he intituled "Paradise
Lost" only a *poem*, yet calls it himself *heroick song*.
Dryden, petulantly and indecently, denies the heroism of
20 Adam, because he was overcome; but there is no reason
why the hero should not be unfortunate, except established
practice, since success and virtue do not go necessarily
together. Cato is the hero of Lucan; but Lucan's authority will not be suffered by Quintilian to decide. However,
if success be necessary, Adam's deceiver was at last
crushed; Adam was restored to his Maker's favour, and
therefore may securely resume his human rank.

After the scheme and fabrick of the poem, must be considered its component parts, the sentiments and the
30 diction.

The *sentiments*, as expressive of manners, or appropriated to characters, are, for the greater part, unexcep-
tionably just.

Splendid passages, containing lessons of morality, or
precepts of prudence, occur seldom. Such is the original

formation of this poem, that as it admits no human manners till the Fall, it can give little assistance to human conduct. Its end is to raise the thoughts above sublunary cares or pleasures. Yet the praise of that fortitude, with which Abdiel maintained his singularity of virtue against the scorn of multitudes, may be accommodated to all times; and Raphael's reproof of Adam's curiosity after the planetary motions, with the answer returned by Adam, may be confidently opposed to any rule of life which any poet has delivered.   10

The thoughts which are occasionally called forth in the progress, are such as could only be produced by an imagination in the highest degree fervid and active, to which materials were supplied by incessant study and unlimited curiosity. The heat of Milton's mind might be said to sublimate his learning, to throw off into his work the spirit of science, unmingled with its grosser parts.

He had considered creation in its whole extent, and his descriptions are therefore learned. He had accustomed his imagination to unrestrained indulgence, and his con- 20 ceptions therefore were extensive. The characteristick quality of his poem is sublimity. He sometimes descends to the elegant, but his element is the great. He can occasionally invest himself with grace; but his natural port is gigantick loftiness. He can please when pleasure is required; but it is his peculiar power to astonish.

He seems to have been well acquainted with his own genius, and to know what it was that Nature had bestowed upon him more bountifully than upon others; the power of displaying the vast, illuminating the splendid, enforc- 30 ing the awful, darkening the gloomy, and aggravating the dreadful: he therefore chose a subject on which too much could not be said, on which he might tire his fancy without the censure of extravagance.

The appearances of nature, and the occurrences of life,

did not satiate his appetite of greatness. To paint things
as they are, requires a minute attention, and employs the
memory rather than the fancy. Milton's delight was to
sport in the wide regions of possibility; reality was a
scene too narrow for his mind. He sent his faculties out
upon discovery, into worlds where only imagination can
travel, and delighted to form new modes of existence,
and furnish sentiment and action to superior beings, to
trace the counsels of hell, or accompany the choirs of
10 heaven.

But he could not be always in other worlds: he must
sometimes revisit earth, and tell of things visible and
known. When he cannot raise wonder by the sublimity of
his mind, he gives delight by its fertility.

Whatever be his subject, he never fails to fill the imagination. But his images and descriptions of the scenes or
operations of Nature do not seem to be always copied from
original form, nor to have the freshness, raciness, and
energy of immediate observation. He saw Nature, as Dry-
20 den expresses it, *through the spectacles of books;* and on
most occasions calls learning to his assistance. The garden
of Eden brings to his mind the vale of "Enna," where
Proserpine was gathering flowers. Satan makes his way
through fighting elements, like *Argo* between the *Cyanean*
rocks, or *Ulysses* between the two *Sicilian* whirlpools, when
he shunned *Charybdis* on the *larboard.* The mythological
allusions have been justly censured, as not being always
used with notice of their vanity; but they contribute
variety to the narration, and produce an alternate exercise
30 of the memory and the fancy.

His similes are less numerous, and more various, than
those of his predecessors. But he does not confine himself within the limits of rigorous comparison: his great excellence is amplitude, and he expands the adventitious
image beyond the dimensions which the occasion required.

Thus, comparing the shield of Satan to the orb of the Moon, he crowds the imagination with the discovery of the telescope, and all the wonders which the telescope discovers.

Of his moral sentiments it is hardly praise to affirm that they excel those of all other poets; for this superiority he was indebted to his acquaintance with the sacred writings. The ancient epick poets, wanting the light of Revelation, were very unskilful teachers of virtue: their principal characters may be great, but they are not amiable. The reader may rise from their works with a greater degree of active or passive fortitude, and sometimes of prudence; but he will be able to carry away few precepts of justice, and none of mercy.

From the Italian writers it appears, that the advantages of even Christian knowledge may be supposed in vain. Ariosto's pravity is generally known; and though the " Deliverance of Jerusalem " may be considered as a sacred subject, the poet has been very sparing of moral instruction.

In Milton every line breathes sanctity of thought, and purity of manners, except when the train of the narration requires the introduction of the rebellious spirits; and even they are compelled to acknowledge their subjection to God, in such a manner as excites reverence, and confirms piety.

Of human beings there are but two; but those two are the parents of mankind, venerable before their fall for dignity and innocence, and amiable after it for repentance and submission. In their first state their affection is tender without weakness, and their piety sublime without presumption. When they have sinned, they shew how discord begins in mutual frailty, and how it ought to cease in mutual forbearance; how confidence of the divine favour is forfeited by sin, and how hope of pardon may be obtained by penitence and prayer. A state of innocence we can only

conceive, if indeed, in our present misery, it be possible to
conceive it; but the sentiments and worship proper to a
fallen and offending being, we have all to learn, as we have
all to practise.

The poet, whatever be done, is always great. Our progenitors, in their first state, conversed with angels; even
when folly and sin had degraded them, they had not in
their humiliation *the port of mean suitors;* and they rise
again to reverential regard, when we find that their prayers
10 were heard.

As human passions did not enter the world before the
Fall, there is in the " Paradise Lost " little opportunity for
the pathetick; but what little there is has not been lost·
That passion which is peculiar to rational nature, the anguish arising from the consciousness of transgression, and
the horrours attending the sense of the Divine Displeasure,
are very justly described and forcibly impressed.   But the
passions are moved only on one occasion; sublimity is the
general and prevailing quality in this poem; sublimity
20 variously modified, sometimes descriptive, sometimes argumentative.

The defects and faults of " Paradise Lost," for faults
and defects every work of man must have, it is the business
of impartial criticism to discover.   As, in displaying the excellence of Milton, I have not made long quotations, because
of selecting beauties there had been no end, I shall in the
same general manner mention that which seems to deserve
censure; for what Englishman can take delight in tran-
scribing passages, which, if they lessen the reputation of
30 Milton, diminish in some degree the honour of our country?

The generality of my scheme does not admit the frequent
notice of verbal inaccuracies; which Bentley, perhaps better
skilled in grammar than in poetry, has often found, though
he sometimes made them, and which he imputed to the obtrusions of a reviser whom the author's blindness obliged

him to employ. A supposition rash and groundless, if he thought it true; and vile and pernicious, if, as is said, he in private allowed it to be false.

The plan of "Paradise Lost" has this inconvenience, that it comprises neither human actions nor human manners. The man and woman who act and suffer, are in a state which no other man or woman can ever know. The reader finds no transaction in which he can be engaged; beholds no condition in which he can by any effort of imagination place himself; he has, therefore, little natural curiosity or 10 sympathy.

We all, indeed, feel the effects of Adam's disobedience; we all sin like Adam, and like him must all bewail our offences; we have restless and insidious enemies in the fallen angels, and in the blessed spirits we have guardians and friends; in the Redemption of mankind we hope to be included: in the description of heaven and hell we are surely interested, as we are all to reside hereafter either in the regions of horror or bliss.

But these truths are too important to be new; they have 20 been taught to our infancy; they have mingled with our solitary thoughts and familiar conversation, and are habitually interwoven with the whole texture of life. Being therefore not new, they raise no unaccustomed emotion in the mind; what we knew before, we cannot learn; what is not unexpected, cannot surprise.

Of the ideas suggested by these awful scenes, from some we recede with reverence, except when stated hours require their association; and from others we shrink with horrour, or admit them only as salutary inflictions, as 30 counterpoises to our interests and passions. Such images rather obstruct the career of fancy than incite it.

Pleasure and terrour are indeed the genuine sources of poetry; but poetical pleasure must be such as human strength and fortitude may combat. The good and evil

of Eternity are too ponderous for the wings of wit; the
mind sinks under them in passive helplessness, content
with calm belief and humble adoration.

Known truths, however, may take a different appearance, and be conveyed to the mind by a new train of
intermediate images. This Milton has undertaken, and
performed with pregnancy and vigour of mind peculiar to
himself. Whoever considers the few radical positions
which the Scriptures afforded him, will wonder by what
10 energetick operation he expanded them to such extent, and
ramified them to so much variety, restrained as he was by
religious reverence from licentiousness of fiction.

Here is a full display of the united force of study and
genius; of a great accumulation of materials, with judgement to digest, and fancy to combine them: Milton was
able to select from nature, or from story, from ancient
fable, or from modern science, whatever could illustrate
or adorn his thoughts. An accumulation of knowledge
impregnated his mind, fermented by study, and exalted by
20 imagination.

It has been therefore said, without an indecent hyper-
bole, by one of his encomiasts, that in reading "Paradise
Lost," we read a book of universal knowledge.

But original deficience cannot be supplied. The want
of human interest is always felt. "Paradise Lost" is one
of the books which the reader admires and lays down, and
forgets to take up again. None ever wished it longer
than it is. Its perusal is a duty rather than a pleasure.
We read Milton for instruction, retire harassed and over-
30 burdened, and look elsewhere for recreation; we desert
our master, and seek for companions.

Another inconvenience of Milton's design is, that it
requires the description of what cannot be described, the
agency of spirits. He saw that immateriality supplied no
images, and that he could not show angels acting but by

instruments of action; he therefore invested them with
form and matter. This, being necessary, was therefore
defensible; and he should have secured the consistency
of his system, by keeping immateriality out of sight, and
enticing his reader to drop it from his thoughts. But he
has unhappily perplexed his poetry with his philosophy.
His infernal and celestial powers are sometimes pure
spirit, and sometimes animated body. When Satan walks
with his lance upon the *burning marle*, he has a body;
when, in his passage between hell and the new world, he 10
is in danger of sinking in the vacuity, and is supported by
a gust of rising vapours, he has a body; when he animates
the toad, he seems to be mere spirit, that can penetrate
matter at pleasure; when he *starts up in his own shape*,
he has at least a determined form; and when he is brought
before Gabriel, he has *a spear and a shield*, which he had
the power of hiding in the toad, though the arms of the
contending angels are evidently material.

The vulgar inhabitants of Pandæmonium, being *incor-
poreal spirits*, are *at large, though without number*, in a 20
limited space; yet in the battle, when they were overwhelmed by mountains, their armour hurt them, *crushed
in upon their substance, now grown gross by sinning*. This
likewise happened to the uncorrupted angels, who were
overthrown *the sooner for their arms, for unarmed they
might easily as spirits have evaded by contraction or remove*. Even as spirits they are hardly spiritual; for
contraction and *remove* are images of matter; but if they
could have escaped without their armour, they might have
escaped from it, and left only the empty cover to be bat- 30
tered. Uriel, when he rides on a sun-beam, is material;
Satan is material when he is afraid of the prowess of
Adam.

The confusion of spirit and matter which pervades the
whole narration of the war of heaven fills it with incon-

gruity; and the book, in which it is related, is, I believe, the favourite of children, and gradually neglected as knowledge is increased.

After the operation of immaterial agents, which cannot be explained, may be considered that of allegorical persons, which have no real existence. To exalt causes into agents, to invest abstract ideas with form, and animate them with activity, has always been the right of poetry. But such airy beings are, for the most part, suffered only
10 to do their natural office, and retire. Thus Fame tells a tale, and Victory hovers over a general, or perches on a standard; but Fame and Victory can do no more. To give them any real employment, or ascribe to them any material agency, is to make them allegorical no longer, but to shock the mind by ascribing effects to non-entity. In the "Prometheus" of Æschylus, we see *Violence* and *Strength*, and in the "Alcestis" of Euripides, we see *Death*, brought upon the stage, all as active persons of the drama; but no precedents can justify absurdity.
20   Milton's allegory of Sin and Death is undoubtedly faulty. Sin is indeed the mother of Death, and may be allowed to be the portress of hell; but when they stop the journey of Satan, a journey described as real, and when Death offers him battle, the allegory is broken. That Sin and Death should have shewn the way to hell, might have been allowed; but they cannot facilitate the passage by building a bridge, because the difficulty of Satan's passage is described as real and sensible, and the bridge ought to be only figurative. The hell assigned to the rebellious
30 spirits is described as not less local than the residence of man. It is placed in some distant part of space, separated from the regions of harmony and order by a chaotick waste and an unoccupied vacuity; but *Sin* and *Death* worked up a *mole* of *aggravated soil*, cemented with *asphaltus*; a work too bulky for ideal architects.

This unskilful allegory appears to me one of the greatest
faults of the poem; and to this there was no temptation,
but the author's opinion of its beauty.

To the conduct of the narrative some objections may be
made. Satan is with great expectation brought before
Gabriel in Paradise, and is suffered to go away unmolested. The creation of man is represented as the consequence of the vacuity left in heaven by the expulsion of
the rebels; yet Satan mentions it as a report *rife in
heaven* before his departure.   10

To find sentiments for the state of innocence, was very
difficult; and something of anticipation perhaps is now
and then discovered. Adam's discourse of dreams seems
not to be the speculation of a new-created being. I know
not whether his answer to the angel's reproof for curiosity
does not want something of propriety: it is the speech of
a man acquainted with many other men. Some philosophical notions, especially when the philosophy is false, might
have been better omitted. The angel, in a comparison,
speaks of *timorous deer*, before deer were yet timorous, and 20
before Adam could understand the comparison.

Dryden remarks, that Milton has some flats among his
elevations. This is only to say, that all the parts are not
equal. In every work, one part must be for the sake of
others; a palace must have passages; a poem must have
transitions. It is no more to be required that wit should
always be blazing, than that the sun should always stand
at noon. In a great work there is a vicissitude of luminous
and opaque parts, as there is in the world a succession of
day and night. Milton, when he has expatiated in the 30
sky, may be allowed sometimes to revisit earth; for what
author ever soared so high, or sustained his flight so long?

Milton, being well versed in the Italian poets, appears
to have borrowed often from them; and, as every man
catches something from his companions, his desire of

imitating Ariosto's levity has disgraced his work with the
"Paradise of Fools"; a fiction not in itself ill-imagined,
but too ludicrous for its place.

His play on words, in which he delights too often; his
equivocations, which Bentley endeavours to defend by the
example of the ancients; his unnecessary and ungraceful
use of terms of art; it is not necessary to mention, because
they are easily remarked, and generally censured, and at
last bear so little proportion to the whole, that they scarcely
10 deserve the attention of a critick.

Such are the faults of that wonderful performance
"Paradise Lost;" which he who can put in balance with
its beauties must be considered not as nice but as dull, but
less to be censured for want of candour, than pitied for
want of sensibility.

Of "Paradise Regained," the general judgement seems
now to be right, that it is in many parts elegant, and
every-where instructive. It was not to be supposed that
the writer of "Paradise Lost" could ever write without
20 great effusions of fancy, and exalted precepts of wisdom.
The basis of "Paradise Regained" is narrow; a dialogue
without action can never please like an union of the narrative and dramatic powers. Had this poem been written
not by Milton, but by some imitator, it would have claimed
and received universal praise.

If "Paradise Regained" has been too much depreciated,
"Samson Agonistes" has in requital been too much admired. It could only be by long prejudice, and the
bigotry of learning, that Milton could prefer the ancient
30 tragedies, with their encumbrance of a chorus, to the
exhibitions of the French and English stages; and it is
only by a blind confidence in the reputation of Milton, that
a drama can be praised in which the intermediate parts
have neither cause nor consequence, neither hasten nor
retard the catastrophe.

In this tragedy are however many particular beauties, many just sentiments and striking lines; but it wants that power of attracting the attention which a well-connected plan produces.

Milton would not have excelled in dramatick writing; he knew human nature only in the gross, and had never studied the shades of character, nor the combinations of concurring, or the perplexity of contending passions. He had read much, and knew what books could teach; but had mingled little in the world, and was deficient in the know- 10 ledge which experience must confer.

Through all his greater works there prevails an uniform peculiarity of *Diction*, a mode and cast of expression which bears little resemblance to that of any former writer, and which is so far removed from common use, that an un-learned reader, when he first opens his book, finds himself surprised by new language.

This novelty has been, by those who can find nothing wrong in Milton, imputed to his laborious endeavours after words suitable to the grandeur of his ideas. *Our language,* 20 says Addison, *sunk under him.* But the truth is, that, both in prose and verse, he had formed his style by a perverse and pedantick principle. He was desirous to use English words with a foreign idiom. This in all his prose is discovered and condemned; for there judgment operates freely, neither softened by the beauty, nor awed by the dignity of his thoughts; but such is the power of his poetry, that his call is obeyed without resistance, the reader feels himself in captivity to a higher and a nobler mind, and criticism sinks in admiration. 30

Milton's style was not modified by his subject: what is shown with greater extent in " Paradise Lost," may be found in " Comus." One source of his peculiarity was his familiarity with the Tuscan poets: the disposition of his words is, I think, frequently Italian; perhaps sometimes

combined with other tongues. Of him, at last, may be
said what Jonson says of Spenser, that *he wrote no language*,
but has formed what Butler calls a *Babylonish Dialect*, in
itself harsh and barbarous, but made by exalted genius,
and extensive learning, the vehicle of so much instruction
and so much pleasure, that, like other lovers, we find grace
in its deformity.

Whatever be the faults of his diction, he cannot want
the praise of copiousness and variety: he was master of
10 his language in its full extent; and has selected the melo-
dious words with such diligence, that from his book alone
the Art of English Poetry might be learned.

After his diction, something must be said of his *versification*. *The measure*, he says, *is the English heroick verse
without rhyme*. Of this mode he had many examples
among the Italians, and some in his own country. The
Earl of Surrey is said to have translated one of Virgil's
books without rhyme; and, besides our tragedies, a few
short poems had appeared in blank verse; particularly one
20 tending to reconcile the nation to Raleigh's wild attempt
upon Guiana, and probably written by Raleigh himself.
These petty performances cannot be supposed to have
much influenced Milton, who more probably took his hint
from Trisino's "Italia Liberata;" and, finding blank verse
easier than rhyme, was desirous of persuading himself that
it is better.

Rhyme, he says, and says truly, *is no necessary adjunct
of true poetry*. But perhaps, of poetry as a mental operation, metre or musick is no necessary adjunct: it is how-
30 ever by the musick of metre that poetry has been discriminated in all languages; and in languages melodiously
constructed with a due proportion of long and short syllables, metre is sufficient. But one language cannot
communicate its rules to another: where metre is scanty
and imperfect, some help is necessary. The musick of the

English heroick line strikes the ear so faintly that it is easily lost, unless all the syllables of every line co-operate together: this co-operation can be only obtained by the preservation of every verse unmingled with another, as a distinct system of sounds; and this distinctness is obtained and preserved by the artifice of rhyme. The variety of pauses, so much boasted by the lovers of blank verse, changes the measures of an English poet to the periods of a declaimer; and there are only a few skilful and happy readers of Milton, who enable their audience to perceive 10 where the lines end or begin. *Blank verse*, said an ingenious critick, *seems to be verse only to the eye.*

Poetry may subsist without rhyme, but English poetry will not often please; nor can rhyme ever be safely spared but where the subject is able to support itself. Blank verse makes some approach to that which is called the *lapidary style;* has neither the easiness of prose, nor the melody of numbers, and therefore tires by long continuance. Of the Italian writers without rhyme, whom Milton alleges as precedents, not one is popular; what reason could urge in 20 its defence, has been confuted by the ear.

But, whatever be the advantage of rhyme, I cannot prevail on myself to wish that Milton had been a rhymer; for I cannot wish his work to be other than it is; yet, like other heroes, he is to be admired rather than imitated. He that thinks himself capable of astonishing, may write blank verse; but those that hope only to please, must condescend to rhyme.

The highest praise of genius is original invention. Milton cannot be said to have contrived the structure of 30 an epick poem, and therefore owes reverence to that vigour and amplitude of mind to which all generations must be indebted for the art of poetical narration, for the texture of the fable, the variation of incidents, the interposition of dialogue, and all the stratagems that surprise and enchain

attention. But, of all the borrowers from Homer, Milton
is perhaps the least indebted. He was naturally a thinker
for himself, confident of his own abilities, and disdainful
of help or hindrance : he did not refuse admission to the
thoughts or images of his predecessors, but he did not seek
them. From his contemporaries he neither courted nor
received support; there is in his writings nothing by which
the pride of other authors might be gratified, or favour
gained; no exchange of praise or solicitation of support.
10 His great works were performed under discountenance, and
in blindness, but difficulties vanished at his touch; he
was born for whatever is arduous; and his work is not
the greatest of heroick poems, only because it is not the
first.

NOTES.

p. 1, l. 1, already written. *E.g.*, by Anthony Wood in his "Athenæ Oxonienses," by Edward Philips, or Phillips, Milton's nephew (1694), by John Toland (1698), by Jonathan Richardson in his "Explanatory Notes on 'Paradise Lost'" (1734), and by Thomas Birch (1738).

l. 4, Mr. Fenton's elegant Abridgement. Elijah Fenton (1683-1750) was a poet, whose name is remembered mainly through his connection with Pope as one of his assistants in translating Homer. See Johnson's "Life of Pope," Bell's English Classics, pp. 23 and 43 *seq.* with the editor's notes. Compare also Johnson's "Lives," Bohn, ii. 245. Fenton's "Life of Milton" was prefixed to his edition of Milton's "Poetical Works," 1727, and to several subsequent editions.

l. 6, this edition. The edition of the works of English Poets for which Johnson wrote the "Lives." See Introduction, p. xvi. above.

l. 7, descended from. Even Mr. Masson's research has failed to discover anything tangible about "the alleged Miltons of Milton in Oxfordshire" ("Life," i. 8). Johnson's authority is the account given by Edward Philips (Godwin, "Lives of E. and J. Philips," p. 352) who was, perhaps, somewhat of a snob, and a little unduly anxious to magnify the social status of his illustrious uncle. The Rev. Joseph Hunter and subsequent writers have exploded the whole of this story. Milton himself only claimed that he came "ex genere honesto."

l. 11, the White Rose. The White Rose was the badge not only of the House of York but also of the House of Stuart, after the accession of James, Duke of York, to the throne. Was Johnson using the term by prolepsis for the earlier Stuarts? There is scarcely any mention of the House of York in Milton's writings.

l. 12, His grandfather. Mr. Hunter, Mr. Masson, Mr. Hyde Clarke, and other writers have shown that the poet's grandfather was named Richard, not John, and that he was a yeoman and living at Stanton St. John, near Holton, near Shotover

G

Forest in Oxfordshire. This Richard may have been under-ranger of Shotover Forest; he was certainly not the ranger during the reign of Elizabeth. He was heavily fined more than once as a Popish recusant, that is, for non-attendance at his parish church.

l. 16, **scrivener**, one who drew up and engrossed wills, settle-ments, and other deeds. (From O.F. *escrivain*, Low Lat., *scribanus*, a writer or notary.) A scrivener or notary did much of the work of an attorney of to-day; who, by the way, is still in Scotland called a " writer."

l. 17, **many of his compositions.** " In the collection of madri-gals, entitled ' The Triumphs of Oriana,' one is by him, and two well-known psalm tunes, ' Norwich ' and ' York,' are of his composition." (Mrs. Napier's note, " Lives," Bohn, i. 93.)

l. 20, **He had probably.** Johnson uses the expression " to have literature," because he means by " literature," scholarship or learning.

The Latin poem addressed to him is that called " Ad Patrem," Globe edition, p. 610; Aldine, ii. 367.

l. 23, **Caston.** This is a mistake, due to Edward Philips. Another account makes the poet's mother to have borne the name Bradshaw. It is now known however that Milton's mother was Sarah, daughter of Paul Jeffrey, a merchant-taylor of London.

l. 24, **Christopher.** The poet's younger brother was born in 1615, and died in 1693; he was made one of the Barons of the Exchequer, and knighted in 1686. " New judges also here, amongst which was Milton, a Papist (brother to that Milton who wrote for the Regicides) who presum'd to take his place without passing the Test." (Evelyn's " Diary," June 2, 1686.) The brothers seem to have been on good terms although differing in politics and religion. See pp. 52-3.

p. 2, l. 2, **chamber-practice.** That part of a barrister's pro-fessional work which he carries on in his chambers or office; such as advising clients, giving written legal opinions, drawing up deeds, etc.

l. 9, **the Crown-office.** " Crown office " here means the Crown-office of the Court of Chancery. The head of the office was called the Clerk of the Crown, and had to attend the Lord Chan-cellor, either personally or by deputy. He made the writs for summoning Parliament, and for the election of members, also the commissions for holding assizes and other commissions. The office was abolished soon after the Revolution. The " secon-dary " mentioned in l. 10, was apparently the Deputy to the Clerk of the Crown.

l. 10, **John and Edward.** Johnson, following Wood (" Fasti

Oxonienses," Bliss, ii. 481), puts the names in the wrong order.
Edward was the elder, John the younger. Edward Philips
(born 1630-1, date of death uncertain,) prefixed a life of his uncle
to the edition of Milton's "Letters of State," published in 1694.
It is one of the principal authorities for the events of Milton's
life. This has been reprinted as an appendix to Godwin's
"Lives of Edward and John Philips" (1815). Edward Philips
wrote other works, including "Mysteries of Love and Eloquence" (1658); "A New World of English Words, or a
General Dictionary" (1658), based on Blount's "Glossographia
Anglicana;" and "Theatrum Poetarum, or a Complete Collection of the Poets . . . With some Observations and Reflections
upon many of them" (1675). See notes on pp. 92, 94.

l. 14, the "Spread Eagle." Formerly most shops and offices
had signs. In the eighteenth century they began to be confined
to taverns. The eagle with extended wings was the crest of the
Milton family.

l. 18, Thomas Young. A Scotchman, and a Puritan. He was
one of the authors of "Smectymnuus," see p. 12. He was made
Master of Jesus College, Cambridge, by the Puritans (in contra-
vention of the statutes) in 1644. He conformed in 1662, and
died Vicar of Stowmarket in Suffolk.
Milton's fourth Latin Elegy, written at the age of 18, is
dedicated to Young. Globe, p. 586, Aldine ii. 333.

l. 22, St. Paul's School. Founded in 1509-12 by Dr. Colet,
Dean of St. Paul's, at the east side of St. Paul's Churchyard.

l. 23, Mr. Gill. This was Alexander Gill, of Corpus Christi
College, Oxford (1564-1635), who was high master of St. Paul's
School for 1608 to 1635. His son, also named Alexander (1597-
1642), was at first a schoolfellow of Milton, and then usher at
St. Paul's. When he went to Oxford Milton corresponded with
him. In 1635 this younger Alexander Gill succeeded his
father as high-master. Both were Puritans in doctrine and
sympathy.

l. 24, entered a sizar. We should now say, entered *as* a
sizar. A sizar at Cambridge is a student who pays lower fees to
his college, and receives his "sizes" or allowances of bread,
butter, etc., free. Originally the sizars, like the servitors at Oxford,
performed certain menial duties for the pensioners, in fact acted
as fags for them. Johnson here makes a mistake, for Milton
was entered as a "lesser pensioner," that is, as an ordinary
student. See Masson, "Life," i. 75-76.

l. 28, Politian. Angelo Poliziano (1454-1494), was one of the
most brilliant scholars of the Italian Renascence. He is considered one of the greatest of modern Latin poets, while his
vernacular poetry, and especially his "Orfeo" (said to be the

"earliest represented drama, not of a religious nature, in a modern language "), holds an important place in the history of Italian literature. See Hallam, "History of Literature," i. 194, 197, and 214.

Dr. Johnson, before his coming to London, prepared to publish by subscription an annotated edition of Politian's Latin poems. See Boswell's " Life," Bohn, i. 54.

l. 81, **his vernal fertility.** His youthful ease in writing poetry.

l. 82, **Cowley.** Abraham Cowley (1608-1667), published his "Poetical Blossoms " in 1633, at the age of fifteen. Cf. Johnson's "Lives of the Poets," Bohn, i. 5, where, however, Johnson (wrongly) gives Cowley's age as thirteen.

p. 3, l. 2, **two Psalms.** Owing to the disuse of ecclesiastical chanting by the Puritans, metrical versions of the Psalms were in demand. For Milton's versions of Psalms 114 and 136, see the Globe edition, pp. 477, *seq.*, Aldine, i, 1. He also did about a dozen of the other Psalms into metre at a later period of his life. See Globe, pp. 535-574, Aldine ii. 327.

l. 6, **his elegies.** Globe, pp. 582, *seq.*

l. 9, **Mr. Hampton.** James Hampton (died 1778), of Christ Church, Oxford, published his translation of the "History of the Greek Polybius," in 1756-1761. It was reviewed by Dr. Johnson in the "Literary Magazine," Boswell, Bohn, iv. 340.

On Milton's Latin poetry, see Mark Pattison, "Milton," p. 41.

l. 13, **Haddon.** Dr. Walton Haddon (1516-1572), Professor of Civil Law at Cambridge and afterwards President of Magdalen College, Oxford. His "Lucubrationes " were published in 1567. He imitated Cicero, " but without catching his manner, or getting rid of the florid, semi-poetical tone of the fourth century." (Hallam, "History of Literature," ii. 82.) When Queen Elizabeth was asked whether she preferred Haddon or Buchanan as men of learning, she replied, " Buchananum omnibus antepono, Haddonum nemine postpono."

l. 13, **Ascham.** Roger Ascham (1515-1568) Greek reader at St. John's College, Cambridge, and for two years tutor to Elizabeth. He was Latin Secretary in succession to Edward VI., Mary, and Elizabeth. His Latin Epistles and Poems (1578) are almost forgotten ; but his " Toxophilus " (1584) and "Schoolmaster" (1570), are still interesting and readable. Johnson once wrote a "Life of Ascham." See Boswell, Bohn, i. 369.

l. 17, **Alabaster's "Roxana."** William Alabaster (1567-1640), was an eccentric and learned scholar of Trinity College, Cambridge, who also had a great reputation as a Latin poet. His tragedy of " Roxana " was acted in the hall of Trinity

College some forty years before its publication in 1632. He wrote a "Lexicon Pentaglotton" of Hebrew, Chaldaic, Syriac, Talmudic Hebrew, and Arabic (1637). It is founded, as Hallam discovered, on the "Dalida" of Groto, an Italian dramatist of the previous century. ("History of Literature," iii. 278.)

Hallam (it may be remarked) places May's continuation of Lucan's "Pharsalia" higher than any Latin verse written by English writers before Milton.

l. 20, some were published. They were published in 1674. See p. 47 above.

l. 28, with no great fondness. See Masson's "Life," i. 159-161.

l. 28, publick indignity of corporal punishment. Aubrey is the authority. But although there is no reason to doubt Aubrey's accuracy or good faith, his statement is only (to use Pattison's Johnsonian language), in the form of a "dubitative interlineation in his MS." The actual words are "whipt him." Most modern biographers seem unnecessarily scandalized by the story; but as corporal punishment (in spite of Johnson's assertion) existed at Cambridge well into the reign of Charles II., there is nothing intrinsically improbable in it.

Dr. Garnett remarks that Aubrey probably only meant that Milton's tutor "on some occasion struck or beat his pupil." It will be remembered that as late as 1747 Goldsmith was beaten, or knocked down in his rooms by his tutor at Trinity College, Dublin, for an infraction of discipline.

Milton's tutor was William Chappell, afterwards Bishop of Cork, who was in the language of the Puritans an "Arminian," that is, not a bigoted Calvinist, but belonging to the more liberal school of theology, of which Laud, Chillingworth, and Taylor were in different ways the exponents. That Chappell was a pedant and exaggerated his authority, is likely enough. On "Arminianism," see pp. 50, 188.

l. 38, verses to Diodati. The first Latin elegy, Globe, p. 582.

Charles Diodati (died 1638), Milton's schoolfellow, was the son of a foreign physician settled in England. The family had left Italy in consequence of their Protestantism. The uncle of Charles, Jean Diodati, was a distinguished Calvinistic divine, and preached at Geneva. Milton's friend practised medicine for some years before his death, at the age of about thirty, in 1638. See pp. 9, 92.

p. 4, l. 14, He declares. The line which Johnson renders is the sixth in the quotation on p. 4. It "obviously means nothing but a repugnance to the observation of those petty formalities and rules which irritate and insult great minds; it is absurd to construe it to have been capital punishment." (Sir Egerton Brydges, "Life of Milton," p. 9 ; quoted by Cunningham.)

It is noteworthy that although Milton was rusticated, or sent down for a term, he was permitted to return in time to keep the Easter term, and he was allowed to change his tutor, and became a pupil of Tovey, instead of Chappell. This seems to show that the college authorities did not entirely sympathize with Chappell in the matter.

l. 80, **inscribed to Hartlib.** Milton's pamphlet "Of Education " (1644), takes the form of a letter addressed to Samuel Hartlib, an ingenious theorist who wrote works on agriculture and education. Hartlib was of Polish origin, and came to England at the beginning of the reign of Charles I. After spending his fortune in his agricultural experiments, he received a pension from Cromwell. To him were dedicated a couple of Sir William Petty's early pamphlets on Economics. His "Reformation of Schools " is based on the doctrines of his fellow-countryman, Kommensky or Commenius, the great educational reformer.

Milton's "Letter to Hartlib " will be found in the Bohn edition of Milton's "Prose Works," iii. 462, seq.

l. 84, **"On the likeliest Way to Remove Hirelings."** Milton's "Prose Works," Bohn, iii. 1 seq. It is curious that preceding editors of this "Life of Milton " have not noticed that Johnson's quotation is far from verbally exact. Milton says nothing at all about "the profits of lands forfeited by the act for superstitious uses." These words are added by Johnson himself. Milton is talking of the expenses of properly educating ministers and teachers. He says : " But be the expense less or more, if it be found burdensome to the Churches, they have in this land an easy remedy in their recourse to the civil magistrate ; who hath in his hands the disposal of no small revenues, left perhaps anciently to superstitious, but meant undoubtedly to good and best uses ; and therefore, once made public, applicable by the present magistrate to such uses as the church, or solid reason from whomsoever, shall convince him to think best. And those uses may be, no doubt, much rather than as glebes and augmentations are now bestowed, to grant such requests as those of the churches : or to erect in greater number, all over the land, schools, and competent libraries to those schools, where languages and arts may be taught free together, without a needless, unprofitable, and inconvenient removing to another place. So all the land would be soon better civilized, and they who are taught freely at the public cost might have their education given them on this condition, that therewith content, they should not gad for preferment out of their own country, but

continue there thankful for what they received freely, bestowing
it as freely on their country, without soaring above the meanness
wherein they were born.   But how they shall live when they
are thus bred and dismissed, will be still the sluggish objection.
To which it is answered, that those public foundations may be
so instituted, as the youth therein may be at once brought up to a
competence of learning and to an honest trade; and the hours of
teaching so ordered, as their study may be no hindrance to their
labour or other calling " (p. 27). The clause in p. 5, ll. 4-7 above
(" by which means " to the end) is not in Milton.

The proper title of the pamphlet runs: "Considerations touching the likeliest Means to Remove Hirelings out of the Church."

p. 5, l. 8, **One of his objections.**   Milton was seldom above
complying with the prejudices of the audience which he might
be addressing. Himself an admirer of Shakespeare and Jonson,
he assumes the intolerance of the vulgar Puritan when a controversial point can be made by doing so.   Thus in the
" Eikonoklastes " he covertly sneers at Charles for his acquaintance with Shakespeare, and calls Sidney's " Arcadia " " a vain,
amatorious poem " not to be " read at any time without due
caution " (" Prose Works," Bohn, i. 326-28).

Plays, as is well known, were constantly acted at the universities.   At Cambridge the hall of Trinity College was the usual
theatre ; but, in the time of Elizabeth, we hear of plays in the
ante-chapel of King's College.   " The last dramatic performance
at either university was, it is said, 'The Grateful Fair,' written
by Christopher Smart, and represented at Pembroke College,
Cambridge, about 1747 " (Note in Murphy's edition of Johnson's
" Works ").

The quotation given is from the " Apology for Smectymnuus,"
" Prose Works," Bohn, iii. 114. What follows is worth quoting as
an example of the bitterness of the Puritan controversialist, as well
as of the lofty self-consciousness of the superior undergraduate.
" There, while they acted and over-acted, among other young
scholars, I was a spectator ; they thought themselves gallant
men, and I thought them fools ; they made sport and I laughed ;
they mispronounced and I misliked ; and to make up the
Atticism, they were out and I hissed. . . For if it be unlawful
to sit and behold a mercenary comedian personating that which
is least unseemly for a hireling to do, how much more blameful
is it to endure the sight of as vile things [as the ' Tempest ' ?]
acted by persons either entered, or presently to enter, into the
ministry ; and how much more foul and ignominious for them
to be the actors ? "

l. 12, **Trinculos.** This probably refers to Shakespeare's " Tempest," and the reference is quite in keeping with Milton's con-

troversial acerbity. But the anonymous annotator in Murphy's-
edition of "Johnson" says, "By the mention of this name he
evidently refers to 'Albemazor,' acted at Cambridge in 1614."

l. 17, **pleasures of the theatre.** Elegia Prima, Globe, pp.
582-83. Compare also "L'Allegro," 131 *seq.*; "Il Penseroso,"
97 *seq.*

l. 20, **entering into the Church.** The Church means here
the ministry of the Church, the clerical state. A man enters
the Church, in the more exact sense of the term, by baptism;
he enters the ministry by ordination.

l. 21, **he declared.** "Reason of Church Government argued
against Prelacy," Milton's "Prose Works," Bohn, ii. 482.

l. 22, **subscribe slave.** Write himself down as a slave.

l. 24, **that could retch.** Unless his conscience could throw it
off lightly.

l. 29, **the articles.** It is curious to note that Milton, when
he wrote this (1641), had already twice subscribed the Thirty-
nine Articles, viz., at the time he took his degrees (B.A. and
M.A.), and was not, therefore, exactly in a position to speak in
such a disengaged manner of others who did the same thing.
Probably, as Johnson suggests, his objection was rather to the
oath of canonical obedience, than to the doctrinal statements
of the articles.

p. 6, l. 1, **in a letter.** This letter is now in the Library of
Trinity College, Cambridge. It bears no date, and no address:
but seems to have been written in 1631 or 1632. See Masson's
"Life," i. 323 [ed. 1881] where the letter is given in full.

l. 10, **When he left the university.** In 1632, after taking
his M.A. degree.

l. 11, **Horton,** a small village in Bucks, a few miles to the
south of Colnbrook, and to the north of Wraysbury station, on
the London and South Western Railway to Windsor.

l. 17, **Masque of "Comus."** A masque was an entertainment
introduced from Italy in the time of Henry VIII. See Morley's
"First Sketch of English Literature," p. 298. The name
"Comus" was not given to the piece by Milton himself. When
it was first printed (in 1637) is was called simply "A Maske.
Presented at Ludlow Castle, 1634, on Michaelmas Night."
This edition was put forth by Henry Lawes (died 1662) the
musician, brother of the still more noted composer, William
Lawes, with a dedication to Lord Brackley, eldest son of the
Earl of Bridgewater. Henry Lawes had composed the music
for the Masque, and had taken part in the performance. On
"Comus," see Masson in the Globe edition, p. 427.

l. 18, **Lord President of Wales.** The office of Lord President
of Wales was established in 1478 by Edward IV., and the official

seat of the President fixed at Ludlow. This arrangement was confirmed in 1536 when Wales was incorporated with England; and was not abolished till 1689. In 1634 the Lord President was John Egerton, Earl of Bridgewater.

Ludlow is in Shropshire, close on the Herefordshire border. In the Castle Butler wrote the first three cantos of "Hudibras" while Secretary to the Earl of Carberry, Lord President after the Restoration.

l. 20, **derived from Homer's Circe.** There is no need to go back to the "Odyssey." The plot is derived partly from an accident which had happened to the children of the Lord President of Wales, who had been actually benighted in Haywood Forest, and partly, as Cunningham points out, from Peele's play, "The Old Wives' Tale" (1595).

l. 23, **a quo ceu fonte.** Ovid, "Amores," lib. iii., eleg. ix., 25. Ovid himself applies this to Homer.

l. 25, **"Lycidas."** This was the last piece in the volume of memorial poems, entitled "Justa Edovardo King," published 1638. It contained poems in Greek, Latin, and English. See Globe, pp. 429, *seq.*

Edward King died by shipwreck, crossing from Chester to Ireland, in August, 1637.

l. 33, **by some lines,** viz., 113-131.

p. 7, l. 2, **"Arcades."** This was "part of an entertainment presented to the Countess Dowager of Derby at Harefield by some Noble Persons of her Family." It was probably written about 1634, and was first published in January, 1645-6. See Masson in Globe edition, p. 410, *seq.*

l. 4, **Harefield,** in Middlesex, four miles from Uxbridge. To the same lady, Alice Spencer, afterwards Countess Dowager of Derby, Spenser had dedicated his "Tears of the Muses" (1591).

l. 8, **the Inns of Court.** The name properly belongs to certain societies, or colleges, of barristers and law-students existing in London, viz., the Inner Temple, the Middle Temple, Lincoln's Inn, and Gray's Inn.

l. 9, **death of his mother.** She died on April 3rd, 1637, at Horton. There is a monument to her in the church of that village.

l. 10, **Sir Henry Wotton's directions.** Sir Henry Wotton (1568-1639) was a scholar, poet, and diplomatist. He was ambassador at Venice and elsewhere from 1604 to 1624. On his return to England he took holy orders, and was made Provost of Eton. His life, written by Izaak Walton, was prefixed to the "Reliquiæ Wottonianæ" (1651).

Wotton's letter to Milton is given by Masson, "Life," i. 737.

l. 15, **Lord Scudamore.** Sir John Scudamore (died 1671), created Viscount Scudamore in 1628, English ambassador at Paris in the reign of Charles I.

l. 16, **Grotius.** Hugo Grotius (1583-1645), scholar, lawyer, and theologian, one of the most learned men of his age. He was born at Delft; his real name was Van Groot, which was latinized in the usual fashion of the age. His famous treatise, "De Jure Belli ac Pacis" (1625), is the foundation of the science of international law. His theological writings were marked by great fairness, and a strong desire to reconcile the difference between Catholics and Protestants. He was drawn towards Laud and the High Church party in the Church of England by their liberality, when compared with the Calvinists and the extreme Roman Catholics.

l. 17, **Christina,** daughter of Gustavus Adolphus, and Queen of Sweden from 1632 to 1654, when she resigned the throne. She was a very eccentric woman, and took great pride in her patronage of men of letters. She was the patron of Descartes and Salmasius (see p. 105), as well as Grotius. She turned Roman Catholic, and died at Rome in 1689.

l. 21, **at Florence.** Milton was at Florence during August and September, 1638.

l. 22, **the academies.** The Italian academies were the outcome of the Renascence. One of the earliest was the Academia Platonica, founded by Lorenzo de' Medici, in 1474. More famous was the Accademia della Crusca, established at Florence in 1582. They were literary and artistic societies which published editions of classical authors and dictionaries, while in their periodical meetings members discussed philosophical and critical difficulties, and read their own compositions to each other.

l. 25, **says he.** "Reason for Church Government," bk. ii., "Prose Works," Bohn, ii. 477-478. The whole passage is full of dignified egotism.

p. 8, l. 2, **Carlo Dati,** a scholar and historian, at the time of Milton's visit to Florence was only nineteen. He left no work of any great importance.

l. 3, **tumid lapidary style,** the exaggerated style of inscriptions on tombs. As Johnson said, in the hearing of Dr. Burney, "In lapidary inscriptions a man is not upon oath" (Boswell, Bohn, ii. 869). Dati's Latin address (prose) is given in the Globe edition, p. 581.

l. 4, **Francini.** Another minor Florentine writer. See Masson, "Life," i. 780. The ode is given in the Globe edition, p. 579.

l. 9, **Holstenius.** Lucas Holstein (died 1661), a learned German, had taken up his residence at Rome as secretary to Cardinal

Barberini, and a librarian at the Vatican. There is a letter of
Milton to Holstenius, see " Prose Works," Bohn, iii. 498.

l. 11, **Cardinal Barberini.** This was Francesco Barberini
(1597-1675), a member of a family which gave several cardinals
to the Church, had great influence at the Papal court, and founded
the Barberini library. He was noted for his patronage of literary
men.

l. 13, **Selvaggi.** " Who Selvaggi was I have not been able to
ascertain." Masson, " Life of Milton," i. 754 (ed. 1859).

l. 14, **Salsilli.** Identified by Mr. Masson with " Giovanni
Salzilli, a poet not mentioned in any of the histories of Italian
literature " (" Life of Milton," i. 754, ed. 1859).

l. 14, **tetrastick.** A tetrastick (or tetrastich), is a stanza of
four lines, just as a distich is one of two.

l. 21, **to publish them.** The verses by Francini, Salsilli,
Selvaggi, and Manso are given in the Globe edition, pp. 578,
seq.; Milton's Latin verses to Salsilli and Manso are given in
Globe edition, pp. 614, *seq.*; Aldine, ii. 371.

l. 28, **he says.** See the Latin note prefixed to the " Testi-
monia," Globe, p. 578 ; Aldine, ii. 325.

l. 29, **on to Naples.** In November, 1638. Nothing is known
of the hermit.

l. 31, **Manso.** Giovanni Battista Manso, Marquis de Villa
(1560-1645), who was an old man, " had been for two generations
the Mæcenas of letters in Southern Italy. He had sheltered
Tasso in the former generation, and Marini in the latter."

l. 32, **Tasso.** See p. 144.

p. 9, l. 8, **for the liberty,** *i.e.,* on account of the liberty he had
allowed himself in talking on matters of religion. He had not
observed very strictly Sir Henry Wotton's advice.

Johnson's authority is Philips, " Life," Godwin, pp. 360-361.

l. 14, **Galileo.** Galileo Galilei (1564-1642) had in 1616 got rid
of the charges brought against him on account of his adoption
of Copernican doctrines by submission to the Pope's order not to
" hold, teach, or defend them; " but in 1632 he got into more
serious trouble by his somewhat tactless " Dialogo sopra i due
Sistemii del Mondo," and was examined by the Inquisition,
and perhaps subjected to torture, although nearly seventy years
of age.

In the " Areopagitica," Milton says : " There [viz. in Italy] it
was that I found and visited the famous Galileo, grown old, a
prisoner to the Inquisition, for thinking in astronomy otherwise
than the Franciscan and Dominican licensers thought." This
passage contains a direct *suggestio falsi*, as Galileo was not in
any real sense a prisoner in 1639.

He had indeed been sentenced to confinement during the

pleasure of the Inquisition. But he was at once permitted to
reside in what he calls in one of his letters "the delightful
palace of Trinità di Monte," the residence of the Tuscan ambassador at Rome; after several months he was allowed to return
to his own house, near Florence, the Villa d'Arcetri, where,
under some slight restrictions, he lived unmolested for the rest
of his days.

l. 15, **he was told by Manso.** Philips, "Life," Godwin,
p. 360.

l. 20, **went on to Florence.** He arrived here on the second
occasion probably at the beginning of March, 1639.

l. 23, **having sent away.** See Philips, "Life," Godwin,
p. 361.

l. 25, **metropolis of orthodoxy.** Geneva was the headquarters
of Calvinism.

l. 27, **John Diodati** (1576-1649) was the uncle of Charles
Diodati, Milton's schoolfellow and friend. See p. 85. He was
Professor of Theology after the death of Beza, and translated the
Bible into Italian (1607).

l. 27, **Frederick Spanheim** (1600-1648), Professor of Theology at
Geneva, and afterwards at Leyden. Father of Ezechiel Spanheim,
diplomatist, and writer on numismatics.

l. 35, "**Epitaphium Damonis,**" Globe, p. 617; Aldine, ii. 376.

p. 10, l. 2, **in St. Bride's Churchyard.** See Edward Philips's
"Life of Milton," pp. 362-364.

St. Bride's Church is in the angle between Fleet Street and
New Bridge Street, close by Ludgate Circus. Here Sir Richard
Lovelace was buried (1658). After the Fire the church was
rebuilt by Sir Christopher Wren.

l. 3, **John and Edward Philips.** See p. 88. These were the
sons of the poet's elder sister, Anne, by her husband, Edward
Philips, who was now dead. The boys were at this time about
eight or nine years old.

l. 5, **in Aldersgate Street.** The house is described by Edward
Philips as " a pretty garden house in Aldersgate Street, . . . at
the end of an entry, and, therefore, the fitter for his turn, by
reason of the privacy; besides that, there are few streets in
London more free from noise than that " ("Life," Godwin,
p. 364. Howell in 1657 says that Aldersgate Street "resembled
an Italian street more than any other in London, by reason of
the spaciousness and uniformity of the buildings and straight-
ness thereof, with the convenient distance of the houses "
(Quoted by Dr. Garnett, p. 67).

l. 10, **Let not our veneration.** Recent writers on Milton
condemn this passage as unfair to Milton and discreditable to
Johnson. It is difficult to see why, unless the person of Milton

is to be considered superior to all criticism. Johnson had a great hatred of cant, and he had been himself a schoolmaster; he saw nothing discreditable in Milton's occupation, but he thought the biographers absurd to try and disguise it beneath high-sounding phrases. Compare p. 18.

l. 27, **a formidable list.** See Aubrey, "Collection for the Life of Milton," Godwin, p. 348, and Philips, "Life," Godwin, p. 362. It included many writers whose works are scarcely looked into by the classical scholars of to-day; such as Varro, Columella, Palladius, Cornelius Celsus, Oppian, Dionysius Afer, Quintus Calaber, and Polyænus. Italian and French, Hebrew, Chaldee and Syriac, were studied as well as Greek and Latin; and in Mathematics the boys read "Urstitius his 'Arithmetic,' Riff's 'Geometry,' 'Petiseus his Trigonometry,' Johannes de Sacro Bosco, 'De Sphæra.'"

p. 11, l. 6, **Georgick.** Used here as an adjective. Johnson means works on agriculture, such as the "Georgics" of Virgil and the "De Re Rustica" of Columella.

l. 8, **Cowley.** See note to p. 2, l. 32. Cowley mixed more with the Court than Milton, and hence is supposed by Johnson to have had better means of knowing "what was wanting to the embellishments of life."

l. 10, **the same plan.** For Milton's plan of education, see his "Letter to Hartlib," Bohn, iii. 462 *seq.*, as well as the account given by his nephew Philips.

Cowley's plan is contained in his "Proposition for the Advancement of Experimental Philosophy," Cowley's "Works," 1710, ii. 608.

l. 12, **the knowledge of external nature.** Johnson's position is just the opposite to that of some modern writers on education. Compare, for instance, Herbert Spencer: "Thus to the question we set out with, 'What knowledge is of most worth?' the uniform reply is, 'Science.' This is the verdict on all the counts. . . . Equally at present, and in the remotest future, must it be of incalculable importance for the regulation of their conduct, that men should understand the science of life, physical, mental, and social; and that they should understand all other science as a key to the science of life" ("Education," 1887, pp. 47, 48). Cf. Masson's "Life," iii. 251 *seq.*

l. 25, **Physiological learning,** that is, physical science. "Physiological" is now restricted to mean the science which deals with the bodily functions of living creatures, and particularly animals.

p. 12, l. 6. **Socrates was rather of opinion.** Compare Xenophon, "Memorabilia," I. i.

l. 8, ὅττι τοι, "Odyssey," iv. 392, "Whatever may have happened to thee, whether good or bad, in the dwellings of men."

l. 12, **History of Poetry.** "Tractatulus de Carmine Drama-tico Poetarum Veterum," by Edward Philips (1670). Cunning-ham remarks that "Johnson derived his knowledge of this little volume from Warton's 'Essay on Pope,' i. 208, 4to ed." Lowndes ("Bibliographer's Manual," iii. 1853) mentions some nine or ten other works by Edward Philips, including his "Theatrum Poetarum, or Complete Collection of the Poets" (1675), which is supposed to contain criticisms on Shakespeare and Marlowe by Milton himself. This last mentioned work calls Milton "the exactest of heroic poets," and says that he has "revived the majesty and true decorum of heroic poesy and tragedy" (pp. 113, 114). See Mrs. Napier's important note, Johnson's "Lives," Bohn, i. 110, 111.

By calling the "Tractatulus" "its only genuine product" (l. 12) Johnson apparently wishes to indicate his doubts as to the authenticity of the other works which were attributed to Edward Philips.

l. 21, **fashionable in the Dutch universities.** Dutch may mean German as well as Dutch. The writers mentioned by Philips are "Amesius, Wollebius, etc." (Godwin, "Lives," p. 364). Dr. William Ames (Amesius) was a Puritan clergyman, who, finding his position in the English Church untenable, went abroad and became minister to an English Puritan congregation at Rotterdam, and died in 1633. He wrote "Puritanismus Anglicanus" (1610), a "Medulla Theologiæ," and other works now forgotten. Milton refers to Ames in the "Tetrachorda" ("Prose Works," Bohn, iii. 343). John Wolleb (Wollebius) was a Swiss divine, who died in 1626.

l. 27, **treatise of "Reformation."** "Of Reformation in Eng-land and the Causes that hitherto have hindered it." See "Prose Works," Bohn, ii. 363, seq.

l. 31, **Hall.** Joseph Hall (1574-1656), Bishop of Exeter, and afterwards Norwich, poet, and divine. He was illegally im-prisoned by the Commons in 1641, for protesting against the validity of pretended statutes passed during the enforced absence of the bishops from the House of Lords; he was then heavily fined and his property pillaged, while he was deprived of his see and its income. His best poetry is his "Virgidemiarum, libri VI.," greatly admired by Pope; his "Mundus Alter et Idem" is an ethical work in the form of the narrative of a fanciful journey; he also wrote sermons and controversial works. He was a very moderate theologian, and was suspected by Laud on account of his sympathy with Puritanism, while he was per-secuted by the Puritans because he was a bishop.

His "Humble Remonstrance to the High Court of Parliament" was published in 1640.

l. 33, **six ministers**. Really only five, Stephen Marshall, Edmund Calamy, Thomas Young (Milton's tutor, who was now Vicar of Stowmarket in Suffolk), Matthew Newcomen, and William Spurstow.

p. 13, l. 2, **Usher**. James Usher, "the greatest luminary of the Irish Church" (1581-1656), became Professor of Divinity at Trinity College, Dublin, in 1607, Bishop of Meath in 1623, and two years later Archbishop of Armagh. Like Hall he was a very moderate Episcopalian, and proposed a scheme (not published till after his death) for "The Reduction of Episcopacy to the Forms of Synodical Government received in the Ancient Church." He was buried in Westminster Abbey, and (by special permission of the Lord Protector) with the burial office of the Anglican Church. He is chiefly remembered by his "Annales Veteris et Novi Testamenti" (1650-1654) which fixed the accepted chronology of our reference Bibles. His reply to Smectymnuus was entitled, "The Judgment of Dr. Rainolde's touching the Original of Episcopacy more largely confirmed out of Antiquity" (1641).

l. 3, "**Of Prelatical Episcopacy**" "Prose Works," Bohn, ii. 421-437.

l. 10, **savageness of manners**. Milton's controversial manners were exceptionally savage for a scholar of eminence, even in that age. Compared with such men as Hall and Usher, not to speak of Taylor and Chillingworth, Milton is remarkable for his bitterness of tone and his narrowness of outlook. He is determined to see only one side of the case, to acknowledge no grain of truth on the part of his opponents. "If ye can find, after due search, but only one good thing in prelaty, either to religion or civil government, to king or parliament, to prince or people, to law, liberty, wealth, or learning, spare her, let her live, let her spread among ye till with her shadows all your dignities and honours, and all the glory of the land be darkened and obscured. But, on the contrary, if she be found to be malignant, hostile, destructive to all these, as nothing can be surer, then let your severe and impartial doom imitate the divine vengeance; rain down your punishing force upon this godless and oppressive government, and bring such a dead sea of subversion upon her, that she may never in this land rise more to afflict the holy reformed Church, and the elect people of God " ("Reason of Church Government," Bohn, ii. 508).

It is curious to think that Milton has been held up for admiration as the champion of toleration and liberal culture, while those he attacked have been represented as the slaves of superstition and authority. As a matter of fact, even Laud showed himself far more tolerant of opposing beliefs than Milton. Laud was the patron and friend not only of High Churchmen, but of Jeremy Taylor, and such latitudinarians as Chillingworth and Hales. Moreover Milton indulged in a bitterness and intensity of invective which is all his own. At times he seems to foam at the mouth with the fury of his denunciation. This is how he speaks of the Anglican prelates, under the veil of a decent, though unambiguous, periphrasis: "But they, contrary, that by the impairing and diminution of the true faith [as accepted by Milton and the Calvinist party], the distresses and servitude of their country, aspire to high dignity, rule, and promotion here, after a shameful end in this life (which God grant them), shall be thrown eternally into the darkest and deepest gulf of hell, where, under the despiteful control, the trample, and spurn of all the other damned, that in the anguish of their torture shall have no other ease than to exercise a raving and bestial tyranny over them as their slaves and negroes, they shall remain in that plight for ever, the basest, the lowermost, the most dejected, most underfoot, and downtrodden vassals of perdition" ("Of Reformation in England," Bohn, ii. 419).

l. 11, "**The Reason of Church Government.**" See Bohn, ii. 489-508. It was published late in 1641, or in the January or February, 1642. See Masson, "Life of Milton," ii. 861-862, note.

l. 16, **says he.** The whole of the introduction to the second book of "The Reason of Church Government" has considerable autobiographical interest. It is written in Milton's most lofty and harmonious prose. The passage quoted by Johnson will be found on p. 481 of Bohn's edition of the "Prose Works," vol. ii.

l. 27, **two more pamphlets.** These were "Animadversions upon the Remonstrant's Defence against Smectymnuus" (1641); and "An Apology against a pamphlet called 'A Modest Confutation of the Animadversions,'" etc. They are perhaps the most boisterous and abusive of all Milton's controversial productions. The second was, of course, a rejoinder to the opponent (Robert Hall, son of Bishop Hall), who had attacked the "Animadversions." It is usually cited as "An Apology for Smectymnuus." It was published at the beginning of 1642. "Prose Works," Bohn, iii. 42 seq., 93 seq. See Masson's "Life," ii. 257, 398-409. Even Dr. Garnett is obliged to allow that these five pamphlets on Episcopacy, "considered as argumentative compositions are exceedingly weak."

l. 28, **one of his antagonists.** The above-mentioned Robert

Hall, whose pamphlet, "A Modest Confutation, etc.," is full of slanderous abuse of Milton.

l. 29, **he answers.** "Prose Works," Bohn iii. 111 *seq.*

p. 14, l. 1, **to obtain with me,** to get the better of me.

l. 3, **she and her sister,** the Universities of Cambridge and Oxford.

l. 5, **kecking,** retching.

l. 6, **queasy,** inclined to vomit.

l. 20, **tries to be humorous.** Milton's humour is noisy and artificial, and not always too delicate. Here is a mild specimen from the "Animadversions:" "A man would think you had eaten over liberally of Esau's red porridge, and from thence dream continually of blushing; or, perhaps, to heighten your fancy in writing, are wont to sit in your doctor's scarlet, which through your eyes infecting your pregnant imaginative with a red suffusion, begets a continual thought of blushing; that you thus persecute ingenious men over all your book, with this one over-tired rubrical conceit still of blushing : but if you have no mercy upon them, yet spare yourself lest you bejade the good galloway, your own opiniative wit, and make the very conceit itself blush with spur-galling" (Bohn, iii. 86).

The passage quoted by Johnson will be found in the "Prose Works," Bohn, iii. 135.

l. 21, **some chaplain in hand.** "Some petty subordinate who is being trained up for the priesthood" (Deighton). More probably, as I think, some chaplain entirely dependent on the favour of his patron.

l. 22, **some squire of the body,** some personal attendant.

l. 23, **court cupboard.** A movable cabinet or sideboard, used for the display of plate during a meal. Compare Shakespeare, "Romeo and Juliet," I. v. 8.

l. 25, **ptisical mottoes,** feeble and ineffective maxims. "Ptisical" for "phthisical" from the Greek $\phi\theta\iota\sigma\iota\varsigma$, consumption, decay.

l. 25, **wherever he had them.** A scornful reference, which implies that their origin was not anything to be proud of.

l. 26, **hopping short.** "Which fail to reach the point at which they aim, just as some poor wretch, racked with convulsive fits, fails to make his way to the point to which he would guide his steps ; 'in the measure' is probably used in a twofold sense, (1) = according to the manner and method, (2) with a sarcastic reference to the word in the sense of the stately dance" (Deighton).

l. 29, **thumbring posies.** A posy was a motto engraved in a ring. In the middle ages rings were often worn on the thumb.

H

l. 29, **this section.** This section of the pamphlet.

l. 32, **that "hell grows darker."** " Paradise Lost," ii. 718, 719.

l. 33, **after Reading was taken.** Reading was taken by the Earl of Essex in April, 1643.

p. 15, l. 2, **Mr. Powel.** Richard Powell was a debtor of the poet's father, who had lent him £500. Possibly the poet went down to Oxfordshire to bring back the annual interest, which had been paid for sixteen years to his father. Mary Powell was about seventeen ; whether he had previously made her acquaintance is not known. "If not, his was the most preposterously precipitate of poets' marriages ; for a month after leaving home he presented a mistress to his astounded nephews and housekeeper" (Garnett, "Life," p. 86).

l. 6, **as Philips relates.** "Life," Godwin, p. 866. Johnson's quotation is not verbally exact. Aubrey, thinking of Mary Milton's Cavalier bringing up, says shrewdly, "Two opinions do not well on the same bolster" ("Collection for Life of Milton," Godwin, p. 845).

l. 14, **Lady Margaret Leigh.** Properly Ley. She was the daughter of Sir James Ley, first Earl of Marlborough, and successively Lord High Treasurer and President of the Council, who died in 1629. "This lady, being a woman of great wit and ingenuity had a particular honour for him [Milton], and took much delight in his company, as likewise her husband, Captain Hobson, a very accomplished gentleman " (Philips, "Life," Godwin, p. 867).

Milton's tenth sonnet is addressed to her. Globe, p. 547. Aldine, i. 99.

l. 29, **" The Doctrine and Discipline of Divorce."** Bohn, iii. 169-273. The first edition was issued, not in 1644, as Johnson says, but in 1643. And Professor Masson has shown that it was probably published as early as August 1, 1643 ; so that it must have been written in July, a few weeks after the poet's marriage, and before Mrs. Milton's visit to her old home. If this view be correct, "we have to suppose," as Mark Pattison says, "that Milton was occupying himself with the composition of a vehement and impassioned argument in favour of divorce for incompatibility of temper, during the honeymoon." And the husband was thirty-five, the bride only seventeen. See Pattison's "Life," p. 58.

l. 30, **" The Judgement of Martin Bucer."** Bohn, iii. 274-814. This is a translation of part of a treatise by Bucer, " De Regno Christi," addressed to King Edward VI. in 1557.

Martin Bucer (1491-1551), a German, once a Dominican friar, embraced Protestantism in 1521. He took up an intermediate position between Luther and the more extreme Zwingli. He was invited to England by Cranmer and was made Regius Professor of Divinity at Cambridge, where he died. His views on marriage, like those of some others of the Reformers, were lax; and he joined with Luther and Melancthon in granting to the protestant champion, Philip, Landgrave of Hesse, a permission to have two wives at once.

l. 81, "**Tetrachordon.**" Bohn, iii. 815-433. This third pamphlet on divorce was published in March, 1645. The word tetrachordon means, having four strings; the four strings to Milton's controversial bow are, Genesis, i. 27-28; Deut. xxiv. 1-2; Matt. v. 31-32; 1 Cor. vii. 10-16.

A fourth pamphlet, "Colasterion, a Reply to a Nameless Answer against the Doctrine and Discipline of Divorce," was published in 1645. See Bohn, iii. 434-461.

l. 84, **This innovation,** viz., the doctrine that Christian marriage is dissoluble by the husband for incompatibility of temper.

l. 85, **the clergy.** The clergy were now presbyterians, those clergy of the Anglican church who had refused to accept Presbyterianism had been ejected from their benefices to the number of several thousands.

l. 85, **Assembly at Westminster.** This Assembly of Divines was convoked by Parliament in the summer of 1643. It numbered about one hundred members, who were paid four shillings a day for their services. The need of Scotch assistance to the Parliament stood in the way of moderate counsels, and under the influence of the Scotch Commissioners the Assembly passed a scheme for a rigid Presbyterian system, and issued the "Directory of Public Worship," the "Westminster Confession of Faith," and the "Longer" and the "Shorter Catechisms," all to this day authoritative documents of the Scotch Presbyterian churches.

p. 16, l. 2, **says Wood.** "Fasti Oxonienses," ii. 483.

Anthony Wood, or à Wood (1632-1695), the antiquary, wrote several important works on the history and famous men of the University of Oxford, to which he belonged. The "Athenæ Oxoniensis" and "Fasti Oxoniensis" are very valuable records. See p. 81.

l. 4, **not to have been much written.** A great outcry was, however, made by the Presbyterian party. Amongst the writers who attacked Milton was William Prynne.

l. 6, **the antagonist.** The anonymous author of the "Answer to the Doctrine and Discipline of Divorce," to which Milton replied in the "Colasterion," one of his most contemptuous and abusive pamphlets.

l. 7, "**Serving man turned solicitor.**" Compare "Colasterion," Bohn, iii. 48-7.

The author of the pamphlet was, says Milton, "intimated to
me, and since ratified to be no other, if any can hold laughter,
and I am sure none will guess him lower than an actual serving-
man.   This creature, for the story must on . . . transplanted
himself, and to the improvement of his wages, and your better
notice of his capacity, turned solicitor.   And having conversed
much with a stripling divine or two of those newly-fledged pro-
bationers that usually come scouting from the university, and
lie here no lame legers [*i.e.*, cripples] to pop into the Bethesda
of some knight's chaplainship, where they bring grace to his
good cheer, but no peace or benediction else to his house ; then
made the cham-party [a conspiracy to assist a party in a lawsuit, on condition that the property recovered is divided] he
contributed the law, and both joined in the divinity."

The whole pamphlet is written in the same fashion.   In the
space of one page Milton calls his opponent " an illiterate and
arrogant presumer in that which he understands not," "some
mechanic," " a gross and sluggish, yet a contentious and overweening pretender," and a " puny clerk."

l. 8, **Howel.** " But that opinion of a poor shallow-brain'd
puppy, who upon any cause of disaffection would have men to
have a privilege to change their wives, or repudiate them, deserves to be hiss'd at rather than confuted " (Bk. iv. letter
vii.; Jacobs' edition, p. 569).   In a note Mr. Jacobs points
out that Featley, one of Milton's opponents, was a friend of
Howell.

James Howell (c. 1593-1666), the traveller and author.   He
travelled in France, Italy, and Spain, and had several official
appointments.   In 1642 he became Clerk to the Privy Council.
Two months after he was thrown into prison by the Parliament, and remained there till 1650.   At the Restoration he
was made Historiographer Royal.   He wrote about seventy
works, of which the best known is the " Epistolæ Ho-Elianæ,
or Familiar Letters Domestic and Foreign " (1645-1655).

l. 11, **in two sonnets.**   Sonnets, xi. xii.   Globe, p. 547 ;
Aldine, i. 100-101.

l. 13, **From this time.**   Milton's severance from the Presbyterians was not entirely, or perhaps even principally, due to
their opposition to his views on marriage.   His dislike of any
definite church organization was bound to alienate him from
men who were as rigid in their ecclesiastical system as Laud
was in his.   Compare sonnet, " On the New Forcers of Conscience
under the Long Parliament," Globe, p. 548 : Aldine, i. 109).

l. 21, **young woman of great accomplishments.**   "One of

Dr. Davis's daughters, a very handsome and witty gentlewoman, but averse, as it is said, to this motion." Philips,
" Life," Godwin, p. 369.

l. 23, **endeavour a reunion.** For the use of " endeavour"
with a direct object, see the collect for the Second Sunday after
Easter.

l. 28, **says Philips.** The whole story is taken from Philips.
" Life," Godwin, p. 369, *seq.*

l. 33, **received her father.** After the surrender of Oxford to
the forces of the Parliament in June, 1646, the Powells had to
leave Oxfordshire. " The family estate was only saved from
sequestration by a friendly neighbour taking possession of it
under cover of his rights as a creditor. The family mansion
was occupied by the Parliamentarians, and the household stuff
sold to the harpies that followed in their train ; the malignant's
timber went to rebuild the good town of Banbury. It was impossible for the Powells to remain in Oxfordshire, and Milton
opened his doors to them as freely as though there had never been
any estrangement. Father, mother, several sons and daughters,
came to dwell in a house already full of pupils, with what inconvenience from want of room, and disquiet from clashing
opinions, may be conjectured " (Dr. Garnet, " Life," p. 98). In
a Latin letter to Carlo Diodati, dated April 21st, 1647, Milton
gives vent to a very natural impatience, which was not, however, intense enough to overcome his benevolent hospitality.
" It is often a subject of sorrowful reflection to me, that those
with whom I have been either fortuitously or legally associated
by contiguity of place, or some tie of little moment "—a strange
way, surely, of referring to the relationship of son-in-law—
" are continually at hand to infest my home, to stun me with
their noise and waste me with vexation, while those who are
endeared to me by the closest sympathy of manners, of tastes
and pursuits, are almost all withheld from my embrace either
by death or an insuperable distance of place " (Bohn, iii.
501).

l. 35, **with other Royalists.** Philips tells us that " it was
not only by children that she [Mrs. Milton] increased the
number of the family, for in no very long time after her coming,
she had a great resort of her kindred with her in the house, viz.,
her father and mother, and several of her brothers and sisters,
which were in all pretty numerous ; who, upon his father's
sickening and dying soon after, went away " (" Life," Godwin,
p. 370).

p. 17, l. 1, " **Areopagitica.**" " Prose Works," Bohn, ii. 49-
101. Professor Arber's useful reprint contains the orders of the
House of Commons re-establishing the censorship (1642-43)

against which Milton protested. He had already printed several books without licence on behalf of the Puritans before the war began; and the "Areopagitica" itself was of course without the *imprimatur*. The pamphlet, which was published in November, 1644, takes the form of a speech to the Parliament. "Areopagitica" is an adjective formed from Areopagus, the Mar's Hill of Acts xvii. The council of the Areopagus had in the early history of Athens great dignity, and a large though somewhat indefinite authority. Milton uses it as a classical equivalent for Parliament.

It is interesting to note that when Milton became a Government official he "pounced upon news-writers, and ferreted unlicenced pamphlets for sedition" in the interests of the Council of State.

l. 6, **unable to solve.** It has been at any rate temporarily solved in the liberal sense desired by Milton.

l. 10, **settlement.** Settled government.

l. 21, **we can hang a thief.** "The punishment of grand larceny, or the stealing above the value of twelve pence (which sum was the standard in the time of King Athelstan, eight hundred years ago), is at common law regularly death" (Blackstone, "Commentaries on the Laws of England," bk. iv., ch. 17).

In the seventeenth and eighteenth centuries the number of capital offences had enormously increased. "From the Restoration to the death of George III. no less than one hundred and eighty-seven capital offences were added to the criminal code." Sir W. Blackstone, notwithstanding the natural conservatism of a great lawyer, had in 1765 complained of the terrible frequency of capital punishment in the English law; but matters were still worse after his death.

l. 24, **collecting his Latin and English poems.** "Poems of Mr. John Milton, both English and Latin, compos'd at several times. Printed by his true copies." Published in January, 1646, according to Mr. Masson, though, the date usually given is 1645. This was the first work published by Milton himself which bore his name.

l. 25, **"Allegro" and "Penseroso."** These were written during Milton's residence at Horton, 1632-38. "L'Allegro" means the "cheerful man," and "Il Penseroso" (which should properly be Il Pensieroso) means the "pensive man." Amongst the other contents of the volume were "Arcades," "Comus," and "Lycidas," and, in fact, with two unimportant exceptions, all the poems written by Milton from his boyhood to 1645.

l. 27, **in Barbican.** The Barbican is a street running into

Aldersgate, where Milton was already living. The house was taken in September, 1645.

The name " Barbican " is derived from the French *barbacane*, the outwork of a castle.

l. 31, **says Philips.** " Life," Godwin, p. 370.

p. 18, l. 2, **young fry.** " Fry " means newly-hatched fish ; used contemptuously for young children.

l. 13, **chamber-milliner,** a milliner who works privately in an ordinary room, and not in a shop. Cf. note to p. 2, l. 2. Dr. Skeat considers the word "milliner" to be " almost certainly *Milaner*, a dealer in goods brought from *Milan* in Italy."

l. 18, **he says.** Philips, " Life," Godwin, p. 371. There is no corroboration of this extraordinary story of Philips. See Masson, " Life of Milton," ii. 482.

l. 20, **adjutant-general.** An adjutant is an officer who assists the commanding officer. The adjutant-general is an officer attached to the staff of the general commanding, who issues all orders to the troops in the name of his superior, and receives all reports and returns.

Sir William Waller (1597-1668), a member of the Long Parliament, who had served during the Thirty Years' War. He fought with varying fortune in 1642-45, was for a time removed by the Self-denying Ordinance, but afterwards served with success under Cromwell.

l. 28, **house in Holbourn.** Of course, Holborn.

Milton's father-in-law, Mr. Powell, died at the close of 1646 or beginning of 1647, leaving him, in lieu of a marriage portion of £1,000 and some other debts, a small property at Wheatley, in Oxfordshire. In March, 1647, Milton's own father died, and was buried at St. Giles's, Cripplegate. A smaller house would now serve his need, and about Michaelmas, 1647, Milton moved to a house in High Holborn, " among them that open backward into Lincoln's Inn Fields," says Philips (" Life," Godwin, p. 371).

l. 30, **till the king's death.** King Charles was beheaded on January 30th, 1649.

Milton's pamphlet, entitled, " The Tenure of Kings and Magistrates, proving that it is lawful to call to account a tyrant or wicked king, and to depose and put him to death," was published in February. It aims at showing that the Presbyterians, who " of late so much blame deposing " are " the men who did it themselves." " Prose Works," Bohn, ii. 1-47.

l. 34, " **Remarks on the Articles of Peace.**" " Observations on Ormond's Articles of Peace with the Irish Rebels." " Prose Works," Bohn, ii. 189-199. Milton's violent pamphlet was published in May, 1649. It recapitulates the articles agreed on by

James, Earl of Ormond, and the Irish papists, and gives a letter
sent by Ormond to Colonel Jones, Governor of Dublin. It adds
a representation made by the Scots Presbytery at Belfast, which
complains bitterly of the lukewarmness of the "sectarian party
in England" (that is, the Independents) with regard to the
Covenant; and of their trial and execution of the king. The
first part of Milton's remarks deals with Ormond's concession in
a very anti-Irish sense, and denounces toleration against all
Roman Catholics. The second comprises a mild apology for
a limited toleration, denounced by the Presbyterians, and a
defence of the trial of the king. It is written in Milton's most
coarsely contemptuous manner. He exclaims: "And then let
men reflect a little upon the slanders and reviles of these
wretched priests [the Presbyterian clergy of Belfast], and judge
what modesty, what truth, what conscience, what anything fit
for ministers or, we might say, reasonable men, can harbour in
them. For what they began in shamelessness and malice, they
conclude in frenzy," etc., etc. (Bohn, ii. 198).

　p.19, l. 10, "**Icon Basilike.**" On February 9th, four days earlier
than Milton's "Observations on Ormond's Articles of Peace," appeared "Eikon Basilike—the Portraiture of his Sacred Majesty
in his Solitudes and Sufferings." Of this work fifty editions
are said to have been sold in a twelvemonth. Milton compared
its effects on the people to those which followed Mark Antony's
reading the will of Cæsar. It was probably written by the
Presbyterian clergyman, Gauden; though some who have most
carefully sifted the evidence attribute the substance of the book
to King Charles. It is not a mere apology; for instance, it
makes Charles blame himself for the execution of Stafford; a
stroke which a presbyterian divine is hardly likely to have
ventured on. If a forgery, it is a very masterly one.

l. 12, **made Latin Secretary.** Milton was made Secretary
for Foreign Tongues to the Council of State, with a salary of
£289 a year, in March 15th, 1649. He was given rooms in
Whitehall.

Some of his "Letters of State," or dispatches, will be found
translated in the Bohn edition of his "Prose Works," ii. 200-333.

l. 13, **prayer taken from Sidney's "Arcadia."** The passage
will be found in Bohn's edition of Milton's "Prose Works,"
i. 327. Johnson has somewhat curtailed it. It continues:
"and that in no serious book, but the vain amatorious poem of
Sir Philip Sidney's 'Arcadia;' a book in that kind full of
worth and wit, but among religious thoughts and duties not
worthy to be named; nor to be read at any time without good
caution, much less in time of trouble and affliction to be a
Christian's prayer-book."

" We feel," says Mark Pattison, "that the finer sense of the author of ' L'Allegro ' has suffered from immersion in the slough of religious and political faction."

As a matter of fact the prayer does not occur in the body of the " Eikon Basilike" at all, but is one of a few "Private Prayers used by His Majesty in the Time of his Sufferings," which are to be found added as an appendix to some editions of the book.

l. 14, "Iconoclastes." " Eikonoklastes ; in Answer to a book entitled ' Eikon Basilike.' " " Prose Works," Bohn, i. 301-496.

In reference to this book Mark Pattison says with justice: "But Milton is worse than tedious ; his reply is in a tone of rude railing and insolent swagger, which would have been always unbecoming, but which at this moment was grossly indecent."

l. 24, gave to Dr. Juxon. William Juxon (1582-1663), who owed his advancement to Laud, became Bishop of London (1633) and Lord High Treasurer (1636). He was the king's frequent adviser on questions of conscience from the beginning of the Long Parliament till his death. On the Restoration he was made Archbishop of Canterbury.

Bishop Juxon attended the king at his execution, and Charles handed to him on the scaffold a copy of his speech and a copy of his private prayers, often printed at the end of the " Eikon Basilike." The papers were demanded from Juxon by the officers, as Fuller relates in his " Church History."

l. 26, Dr. Birch. Thomas Birch, D.D. (1705-1766), a historical writer of industry and acumen, was a correspondent of Dr. Johnson, who reviewed his " History of the Royal Society," (1756-7) in the " Literary Magazine." A couple of letters from Johnson to Birch are given in Boswell's " Life," Bohn, i. 116, 228. Dr. Birch wrote an " Account of the Life and Writings " of Milton for the folio edition of Milton's prose works, published in 1738.

There is no foundation for the statement that the prayer was interpolated by the regicides.

l. 33, Salmasius. This is the Latinized name used by Claude de Saumaise (1588-1653). He was a Burgundian, a great, though not an elegant scholar, and a Protestant. He became Joseph Scaliger's successor as professor of Polite Learning (that is, classical literature) at Leyden. His greatest work was the " Plinianæ Exercitationes " (1629), a commentary on the summary of ancient scientific knowledge known as the " Polyhistoria " of Solinus, a writer of the third century after Christ. On the invitation of Queen Christina he spent a year in Sweden (1651).

p. 20, l. 1, **hundred Jacobuses.** A Jacobus was a gold coin worth twenty-five shillings, struck during the reign of James I.

Compare Milton's Latin epigram "In Salmasii Hundredam," originally inserted in the "Defensio pro Populo Anglicano," now printed with the Poems (Globe, p. 625; Aldine, ii. 351). There is, however, probably no truth in the story of the hundred Jacobuses.

l. 9, **Defensio Regis.** The "Defensio Regia pro Carolo I." was published in October or November, 1649, in Holland.

l. 10. **was required to write.** "1649-50, Jan. 8. That Mr. Milton do prepare something in answer to the book of Salmasius, and when he hath done itt bring itt to the Councill.— *Order Book of the Council of State.*" Quoted by Cunningham, i. p. 101. Milton's answer was called "Pro Populo Anglicano Defensio;" it was published in March, 1651. Opinions differ as to how far it was successful. Mark Pattison says that, "there is no evidence that it produced any effect upon the public, beyond that of raising Milton's personal credit." Dr. Garnett considers that it had great success, but that this success was chiefly due "to the general satisfaction that Salmasius should at length have met with his match."

l. 11, **that Hobbes declared.** Thomas Hobbes (1588-1679) the philosopher. "They are very good Latin both, and hardly to be judged which is better; and both very ill reasoning, hardly to be judged which is worse; like two declamations, *pro* and *con*, made for exercise only in a rhetoric school by one and the same man" ("Behemoth," Molesworth's edition of Hobbes's "Works," vi. 368, quoted by Professor Deighton).

l. 16, **a foolish allusion.** "Pro Populo Anglicano Defensio." Milton's "Prose Works," Bohn, i. 11.

l. 18, **Salmacis.** A fountain in Caria, near Halicarnassus. See Ovid, "Metamorphoses," iv. 286. This insulting buffoonery is common enough in Milton's controversial works, both Latin and English, and indeed in those of many other scholars of the sixteenth and seventeenth centuries. See Masson, "Life," iv. 262-266.

l. 21, **says Milton.** "Prose Works," Bohn, i. 115. The whole passage is a piece of stupid and clumsy banter. Salmasius had been arguing in favour of monarchy from the example of the lower animals, *e.g.*, bees, quails, and barn-door fowls.

"But leave off playing the fool with bees; they belong to the Muses and hate and (as you see) confute such a beetle as you are. 'The quails are under a captain.' Lay such snares for your own bitterns; you are not a fowler good enough to catch us. Now you begin to be personally concerned. Gallus gallinaceus [the domestic cock] say you 'has both cocks and

hens under him.' How can that be, since you that are Gallus
[the word means Frenchman, as well as cock] and too Gallinaceus
[too much like a cock] cannot, so they say, govern your own
single hen, but let her govern you?" The rest of the passage is
cruder and coarser still.

"Whenever Milton wants to be particularly poignant in his
abuse, and to vary the form of it from sneers at the bad or bald
Latin of Salmasius, or the silliness of his scholarship, he brings
in Madame Salmasius" (Masson, iv. 263).

l. 24, **vitious**, more classical form of "vicious" (*vitiosus*). The
word means faulty, defective.

l. 25, **Persona**. Milton's attack ("Prose Works," Bohn, i.
10) is not quite justifiable; though of course the usage of which
he complains is very infrequent during the best age. See bottom
of p. 21.

Persona meant in turn: (1) a mask used by players; (2) a
personage in a play; (8) metaphorically a part or character
sustained by any one in actual life; (4) personal appearance;
(5) an individual.

l. 28, **solecism**. Impropriety in speaking or writing. It
comes from the Greek σόλοικος, speaking incorrectly, like an inhabitant of Soloi in Cilicia, where Greek was corruptly spoken
(Skeat).

The adjective *solecistical* in the next line is very unusual.

l. 30, **as Ker.** "Selectarum de Lingua Latina Observationum
Libri duo," by John Ker (1709).

The "some one before him" may be Vavassor, "De Epigr."
(1678) cxxii. p. 144, as Mitford pointed out. See Mrs. Napier's
note, Bohn edition of Johnson's "Lives," i. 128.

p. 21, l. 2, **dim of sight.** He had already lost the sight of
one eye.

l. 4, **a thousand pounds.** The statement that Milton received a thousand pounds from the Council of State was
apparently first made by Toland in his "Life of Milton," 1699,
p. 102. But there is no evidence for it. See Masson, "Life,"
iv. 321.

l. 15, **Christina.** See note to p. 7, l. 17. The anecdote about
Christina is probably from the "Journal of the Swedish Em-
bassy," in the years 1653 and 1654, written by the Ambassador,
the Lord Commissioner Whitelocke (1772).

l. 25, **he was dismissed.** In 1652 Salmasius left Sweden of
his own free will. By "dismissed" Johnson probably did not
wish to imply that he was sent away unwillingly.

l. 29, **Restauration.** Unusual spelling so late in the eighteenth
century. Of course from the Latin *restauratio*.

l. 38, **that of Juvenal.** "Sat." iv. 14, 15. Juvenal here, however, seems to use the word "persona" to mean personal appearance rather than an individual.

p. 22, l. 2, **delighted himself.** Milton, "Prose Works," Bohn, i. 222.

l. 4, **the Spa.** Spa, in Belgium, near Liége. The word *Spa* is, from this place, applied to any spring of mineral water used for medical treatment.

l. 5, **controvertists.** This word is now obsolete.

l. 9, **commenced monarch.** Entered upon the rights and duties of a king. This use for the word is now confined to the Universities. "To commence Bachelor of Arts " is to take the degree of Bachelor; "Commencement" at Cambridge is the day on which degrees are conferred.

Cromwell became Lord Protector December 16th, 1653.

l. 16, **to his power,** as far as lay in his power.

l. 23, **blind.** There is a full account of the origin and symptoms of his blindness in a letter of Milton addressed to the Greek, Leonard Philaras, September 28th, 1654. He seems to have suffered either from amaurosis (*gutta serena*), a disease of the optic nerve, which leaves the pupil clear and bright ; or, still more probably, glaucoma, which in its initial stages presents many of the symptoms described by Milton—the halos seen round candles, the clouds, the pain in the eyeballs.

l. 24, **disabled to discharge.** We should say disabled *from* discharging. However, an assistant was given him, and for a time Andrew Marvell held the position. Milton's salary was reduced in April, 1655, from £288 to £150 a year.

l. 26, **to be diverted,** *i.e.*, diverted from his purpose. We seldom use " diverted " in this absolute manner, unless we mean "amused."

l. 28, **About this time.** Milton's first wife died in 1652, in May. A third daughter had been born in that month.

l. 29, **three daughters.** Milton's children by his first wife were a daughter, born in 1646 (Anne, who was deformed and lame); a daughter, born in October, 1648 (Mary); a son, born in March, 1650, who died an infant about six weeks after his mother; and the daughter (Deborah) just mentioned, born in May, 1652. See p. 53 above.

At the time of his first wife's death, Milton was living in Petty France, Westminster, whither he had removed from his official rooms in Whitehall, in December, 1651.

It was, acccording to Philips, "a pretty garden house . . . next door to my lord Scudamore's, and opening into St. James's Park. Here he lived no less than eight years, namely, from the year 1652 till within a few weeks of King Charles II.'s Restoration" (Godwin's "Lives," p. 374). This house, after-

wards known as 17, York Street, was owned by Bentham, who
put on it a tablet with the words, "Sacred to Milton, Prince of
Poets."

l. 31, **after a short time.** In November, 1656—surely a
sufficient delay. Johnson seems to have thought that Milton's
first wife died in 1654 instead of 1652.

l. 33, **within a year.** The second Mrs. Milton died in
February, 1658; her infant daughter (Katherine) died in the
next month. She was buried in St. Margaret's, Westminster.

l. 35, **with a poor sonnet.** This is the beautiful sonnet
beginning, "Methought I saw my late espoused saint" (Globe,
p. 552).

Johnson's capacity for understanding and enjoying lyrical
poetry was absolutely microscopic. See above, Introduction,
p. xxiii.

p. 23, l. 2, **"Apologia pro Rege."** "Polypragmaticus"
means a Busybody.

This pamphlet was written by John Rowland, and was published in 1650. In 1653 the author published a Supplement to
it, called "Polemica."

l. 6, **published an answer.** "Johannis Philippi Angli
Responsio ad Apologiam anonymi cujusdam tenebrionis"
(1652). "Tenebrio," means one who shuns the light, a swindler.

l. 8, **to Bramhal.** John Bramhall (1594-1663), Bishop of
Derry and afterwards Archbishop of Armagh. He was a strong
churchman, and was known as the Irish Athanasius. In 1650
he was living in exile at Antwerp.

l. 11, **Next year.** Johnson means in 1652, which is the correct date. This pamphlet "was a prodigy of scurrilous invective, bettering the bad example which Milton had set (but which
hundreds in that age had set him) of ridiculing Salmasius's
foibles, when he should have been answering his arguments"
(Dr. Garnett.)

l. 12, **Peter du Moulin.** Peter du Moulin, D.D. (died 1684),
born in France, had come to England before 1640, and had
been ordained and made rector of Wheldrake, about eight miles
from York, from which place he was expelled by the Presbyterians in 1644. After the Restoration he recovered his
preferment.

l. 12, **Morus or More.** Alexander Morus or More (died 1670),
a Frenchman, but of Scotch descent, who was professor of
Sacred History at Amsterdam, a friend of Salmasius, and at
that time living in the great scholar's house. More had, as a
matter of fact, corrected the proofs of the "Regii Sanguinis
Clamor." But he soon after quarrelled with Salmasius—the
details of the scandal may be seen in Milton's "Prose Works,"

i. 225, *seq.*, or in a brief form in Dr. Garnett's " Life," p. 118,—
and did his best to escape from Milton's wrath by letting the
poet know that the pamphlet was not written by him.

l. 14, "**Defensio Secunda.**" "Johannis Miltoni pro populo
Anglicano defensio secunda" (1654). A translation will be
found in Milton's "Prose Works," Bohn, i. 214-300.

l. 18, **means of knowing the true author.** This is put too
strongly.

Milton did not know that Du Moulin wrote it, though he
knew that Morus did not write it. See Masson, "Life," v.
222.

l. 25, "**Deserimur, Cromuelle.**" See p. 24 for translation by
Johnson, who appends a footnote to the word "Glorississimus."
"It may be doubted," he says, "whether *gloriosissimus* be here
used with Milton's boasted purity. *Res gloriosa* is an *illustrious
thing;* but *vir gloriosus* is commonly a *braggart*, as in *miles
gloriosus.*"

p. 24, l. 22, **to defend himself.** "Johannis Miltoni Angli
pro ce Defensio contra Alexandrum Morum" (1655), which is
answer to More's pamphlet, entitled "Fides Publica contra
calumnias Johannis Miltoni" (1654).

l. 27, "**Morus es ?**" "Are you Morus or Momus, or indeed,
both at once?" "Morus" means a fool, as well as a mulberry
tree. Momus was the god of jibes and jests.

l. 29, **the known transformation**, viz., that expressed in the
lines inaccurately quoted by Johnson from Ovid, "Metam.,"
iv. 51-2:

"An quæ poma alba ferebat,
Ut nunc nigra ferat contactu sanguinis arbor."

p. 25, l. 2, **Declaration of the reasons for a war with Spain.**
Milton's "Prose Works," Bohn, ii. 338-353.

l. 4, **artfully suspended.** When the negotiations were
delayed for the purpose of securing some advantage.

l. 5, **imputed to Mr. Milton's indisposition.** Whitelocke's
"Memorials," May 6th, 1656, edit. 1732, p. 645. Compare
Masson, "Life," v. 240.

l. 10, **external interruptions**, viz., the needs of controversy.
He retained his secretaryship till 1660.

l. 20, **says Philips.** "Life of Milton," Godwin's "Lives,"
p. 375.

l. 21, **discomposed**, disarranged.

l. 22, **Latin dictionary printed at Cambridge.** "The 'Cambridge Dictionary,' published in quarto, 1693, is a copy, with
some small additions, of that of Dr. Adam Littleton in 1685, by
sundry persons, of whom there is reason to believe that Edward

Philips was one" (Cunningham)⋆ The first edition of "Littleton's Dictionary" was printed in 1678.

l. 23, **folios.** A folio is a book composed of sheets, each of
which is folded only once. The actual size depends on the size
of the sheet. The usual height, however, is about twenty to
twenty-four inches.

l. 26, **but with more,** except with more, etc. Johnson here
preserves the old usage of the negative with *but*, on which see
Mason's "Grammar" (1878), p. 114, note.

l. 29, **Milton's narrative.** "The History of Britain, that
part especially now called England, from the first traditional
beginning continued to the Norman Conquest" (1670). Milton's
"Prose Works," Bohn, v. 164-398. Milton's "History" has no
historical value. See p. 45, l. 8.

l. 33, **long chusing and beginning late.** "Paradise Lost,"
ix. 26.

p. 26, l. 1, **in his verses to Mansus.** See above, p. 91.
The verses to Manso are given in the Globe edition, p. 615.
Johnson refers to vv. 80, *seq.*, thus translated by Cowper:

> " Should I recall hereafter into rhyme
> The kings and heroes of my native clime,
> Arthur the chief, who even now prepares,
> In subterraneous being, future wars,
> With all his martial knights to be restored,
> Each to his seat around the federal board,
> And oh, if spirit fail me not, disperse
> Our Saxon plunderers, in triumphant verse !"

l. 2, **says Fenton.** This is Pope's friend and assistant in
translating Homer, Elijah Fenton (1683-1750). See above,
p. 81.

The "other destiny" to which Arthur was reserved was Sir
Richard Blackmore's epic, "King Arthur," on which see Johnson's "Life of Blackmore," "Lives," Bohn, ii. 223-242.
"Sonorous Blackmore," "who sings so loudly and who sings
so long," was the butt of all the wits of the day.

l. 4, **in a library at Cambridge.** In the library of Trinity
College, Cambridge, to which they were presented in 1736 by
Thomas Clerke, a fellow of the college. To Clerke they had
been given by Charles Mason, another fellow, who had collected
the MSS.

l. 6, **Mysteries.** Mysteries or miracle plays were sacred
dramas founded on the Scripture history in the lives of the
saints. The earliest of which a specimen has come down to us
dates from the fourth or fifth century, and is written in Greek.

There are several Latin plays of this type by Hroswitha, a German nun, in the middle of the tenth century. Miracle plays became common in England from the twelfth century, and were performed as late as the very end of the sixteenth.

The name "mystery" was not given to the plays because they dealt with the "mysteries" of religion, but because they were acted by craftsmen. The word so used represents the Mid. Eng. *mistere*, from French *mestier*, a trade or employment, which itself comes from Lat. *ministerium*.

l. 7, **Philips had seen.** "Life of Milton," Godwin's "Lives," p. 376.

l. 8, **Satan's address to the sun.** "Paradise Lost," iv. 32-41.

l. 9, **consist of allegorical persons.** This is not exactly true. The *dramatis personæ* of the "moralities" were allegorical; those of the "mysteries" were usually real persons, although allegorical persons were occasionally introduced.

l. 23, **Mutes,** that is, non-speaking characters.

l. 33, προλογίζει, prologizes, speaks the prologue.

p. 27, l. 1, **it corrupts not,** does not decay.

l. 4. **exhorts to the sight of God,** exhorts to purity by which alone we may see God (St. Matt. v. 8).

l. 18, **by his name signifying.** The name Gabriel is said to signify "the strength of God," or "the man of God."

p. 28, l. 10, "**Adam unparadised.**" The titles of classical plays frequently took this form, *e.g.,* "Prometheus Vinctus," "Hercules Furens."

l. 12, **frequency.** His frequent visits.

l. 19, **tracing Paradise with a more free office.** Going about Paradise more freely than the angelic guard (the Chorus).

l. 32, **confusedly,** with shame.

l. 32, **in a shape,** in bodily shape.

p. 29, l. 1, **entertains the stage,** occupies the stage.

l. 10, **a mask.** See note to p. 6.

l. 18, **in their seminal state,** in their very beginnings, as the seed is to the plant.

l. 27, **numbers,** poetry.

l. 29, **seemly arts and affairs.** See "Reason of Church Government," Introd. to Bk. II., Bohn, ii. 481.

p. 30, l. 5, "**Cabinet Council.**" "The Cabinet Council or the Chief Arts of Empire Dis-Cabineted. By the ever-renowned Knight, Sir Walter Raleigh, published by John Milton, Esq." (1658). See Masson, "Life of Milton," v. 404-405.

l. 6, "**Treatise of Civil Power.**" Milton's "Prose Works," Bohn, ii. 520-548. It was published in 1659.

l. 7, "**Means of Removing Hirelings**" (1659). Milton's

" Prose Works," Bohn, iii. 1-41. It was published in August, 1659.

l. 9, **Oliver was now dead.** He died September 3, 1658. His son Richard resigned in May, 1659.

l. 10, **extemporary**, provisional.

l. 14, **which Toland has published.** John Toland (1670-1722), one of the chief Deistic writers, the author of "Christianity not Mysterious" (1696), "Nazarenus" (1718), and other unorthodox volumes. His "Life of Milton" was first published in an edition of Milton's prose works, printed at Amsterdam in 1698.

l. 17, **bated no jot of heart.** See Sonnet XXII., the second sonnet to Cyriack Skinner:

> " Yet I argue not
> Against Heaven's hand or will, nor bate a jot
> Of heart or hope, but still bear up and steer
> Right onward."

l. 19, " **A ready and easy way.**" "The Ready and Easy Way to establish a free Commonwealth, and the excellence thereof, compared with the Inconveniences and Dangers of readmitting Kingship in this Nation" (1660).

l. 21, **enough considered**, thought of enough importance.

l. 24, **apparently**, obviously.

l. 25, **Harrington.** James Harrington (1611-1677), the political writer, whose "Oceana" was published in 1656. He founded the Rota Club, a political society which met in Westminster. The ballot (in the virtues of which Harrington had a pathetic trust) decided who were to hold office, and the officers retained their position only for a short time, so there was constant rotation among them. Cyriac Skinner, Milton's pupil and friend, was a member.

In his "Ready and Easy Way to Establish a Free Commonwealth," Milton proposes to do without King or Parliament and confide the government to a Council of State of which one-third retire annually, or better still, at longer intervals—a scheme, he says, "by some lately propounded," which "they call 'partial rotation'" (Bohn, ii. 122).

l. 29, **Notes upon a Sermon.** "Brief Notes upon a Late Sermon, entitled the Fear of God and the King, preached and since published by Matthew Griffith, D.D., and Chaplain to the late King." The sermon was preached at the Mercer's Chapel, on Sunday, March 25, 1660. Long before this the general expectation was that the monarchy would be restored. On March 19, Pepys writes, "All the discourse now-a-day is,

I

that the King will come again ; and for all I see, it is the wishes
of all ; and all do believe that it will be so."

l. 32, **L'Estrange.** Sir Roger L'Estrange (1616-1704), a
pamphleteer and the founder of English journalism, who started
the " London Gazette," in 1666.

l. 32, **petulantly,** saucily, wantonly.

p. 31, l. 2, **was no longer secretary.** He was dismissed in
April, 1660. But he had long ago left his official lodgings
in Whitehall, see p. 108 above.

l. 6, **Bartholomew Close,** a row of old houses, once the west
cloister of the Priory of St. Bartholomew, Smithfield.

Here Milton hid himself from May until the end of August,
1660, when the Act of Oblivion was passed.

l. 9, **every house in which he resided.** The following list
contains the most important residences of Milton from the time
of his return from Italy : St. Bride's Churchyard (1639-1642),
Aldersgate Street (1642-1645), the Barbican (1645-1647), High
Holborn (1647-1649), Whitehall (1649-1651), Petty France, Westminster (1651-1660), Bartholomew Close (1660), Jewin Street
(1661-1663 ?), Artillery Walk, Bunhill Fields (1663 ?-1674).

l. 16, **Act of Oblivion.** The king had, in the Declaration of
Breda (April 14th, 1660), promised a general pardon to all his
subjects save to those who might be excepted by Parliament.
The Bill of Indemnity and Oblivion was debated for some
months in the Convention Parliament. Most of the king's judges
were exempted from pardon in the Act of Oblivion as finally
agreed on (August, 1660), but a special Act of Parliament was
to be passed for their execution. Twenty others were rendered
incapable of holding any office under the crown. Ten persons
were actually put to death at that time, and three others seized
in Holland were executed some time afterwards. The long delay, and the many changes from time to time introduced, caused
a great feeling of uneasiness among those who had taken a pro-
minent part in connexion with the death of the late king. See
Hallam, " Constitutional History," edition 1869, pp. 503-5.

l. 23, **Milton's " Defence."** The " Defensio pro Populo
Anglicano." The copy, now in the British Museum, of the
order to burn this book, is dated August 13th, and includes the
" Eikonoklastes." The order was executed a fortnight later.
Masson, " Life of Milton," vi. 181, 193.

l. 24, **Goodwin's " Obstructors of Justice."** John Goodwin
(c. 1593-1665), a Puritan divine, was one of the most outspoken
of the Independents. He attacked both the theology and the
politics of the Presbyterians. He was, as Calamy said, " a man
by himself, was against every man, and had every man against
him." His " Obstructors of Justice " (1649) takes the same

position as Milton's pamphlets, and defends the execution of
the king. It was burnt by the hangman on August 27th, 1660.
He must not be confounded with Thomas Goodwin (1600-79),
an Independent minister, who was made President of Magdalen
College, Oxford, by Oliver, and attended the Lord Protector on
his death-bed.

l. 29, **August 19**. This should be August 29th, 1660. The
act was called an "Act of Free and General Pardon, Indemnity,
and Oblivion," so that Johnson's loyal enthusiasm over the title
is a little out of place.

p. 32, l. 1, **Burnet thinks**. Gilbert Burnet (1643-1715), Bishop
of Salisbury, the author of a "History of his Own Times," published after his death, 1724-84.

l. 8. **Dalrymple's observation**. Sir John Dalrymple's "Memoirs of Great Britain and Ireland" (1771-88). "This Dalrymple," said Johnson, "seems to be an honest fellow, for he
tells equally what makes against both sides. But nothing can
be poorer than his mode of writing; it is the mere bouncing of
a school-boy" (Boswell's "Johnson," Bohn, ii. 200).

l. 8, **in the House**, sc., House of Commons.

l. 9, **Marvel, Morrice, and Sir Thomas Clarges**. Andrew
Marvell (1621-78), the poet, acted as Milton's assistant in the
secretaryship in 1657. He was elected member for Hull in
Richard Cromwell's Parliament, and again in 1660 and 1661.
According to Philips, he "acted vigorously on his (Milton's)
behalf, and made a considerable party for him" ("Life of Milton," Godwin).

William Morrice, or Morice (died 1676), was a friend of Monk,
and was, it is said, the first confidant of Monk's design to restore
the king. He was appointed Secretary of State in 1660, and
held the post till 1668.

Sir Thomas Clarges (died 1695) was Monk's brother-in-law.
He assisted Monk in bringing about the Restoration. After
that event he took, on the whole, a part against the court.
After the Revolution he sat for the University of Oxford.

l. 11, **particular**, detailed.

Richardson in his Memoirs. Jonathan Richardson (died
1745), a writer and painter. The "Explanatory Notes and
Remarks on 'Paradise Lost,' by Jo. Richardson, Father and
Son. With a life of the Author, and a Discourse on the Poem,
by J. R. Sen" (1734), is the book Johnson refers to. The story
about Davenant is told in the "Life," pp. lxxxix.-xc. It was
the "son," the younger Jonathan Richardson, who was asked
by Pope to find out something about the unknown author of
"London," which had appeared on the same morning as the
"Epilogue to the Satires." See Introduction, p. xi. above.

l. 12, **Betterton.** Thomas Betterton (died 1710) the famous actor.

Davenant. Sir William Davenant (died 1668), the author of "Gondibert" and the "Siege of Rhodes."

l. 20, **if help were wanted,** if additional evidence were required.

The tale is wholly improbable.

l. 26, **Goodwin.** See p. 114, above.

l. 28, **incapacitation.** Goodwin was one of those rendered incapable of holding any office under the crown.

p. 38, l. 6, **in the custody of the serjeant.** "The journals of the House of Commons record that, on Saturday, the 15th of December, 1660, the Sergeant-at-arms was ordered to release Mr. Milton forthwith on payment of his fees, and that on the following Monday, December 17th, on a complaint from Mr. Milton that the fees demanded from Mr. Milton were exorbitant, the matter was referred to the Committee of Privileges, with powers to call Mr. Milton and the Sergeant-at-arms before them and settle the dispute. From another authority we learn that the fees demanded were £150, worth about £500 now, and that the member who brought Mr. Milton's complaint before the House was Mr. Andrew Marvell" (Masson).

He was arrested apparently on the old order of the House of Commons, dated June 16th.

l. 15, **Jewin-street.** This street still exists. It runs off to the east from Aldersgate Street, and is the next turning to the Barbican, where Milton had previously lived. See p. 17. Milton removed to Jewin Street in 1661.

l. 18, **Elizabeth Minshull.** Milton's third wife was the daughter of a Cheshire yeoman, not of a "gentleman." She was a connection of Dr. Paget, Milton's medical attendant, who "recommended" her. She was a girl of twenty-four or twenty-five, while Milton had reached the mature age of fifty-five.

Aubrey calls her "a gentle person, a peaceful and agreeable humour" (Godwin, p. 387). She was pretty and had golden hair, and was accustomed to sing while he accompanied her on the organ and bass-viol. See Masson, "Life," vi. 478, *seq.*

l. 27, **as Philips relates.** This seems to be a mistake of Johnson's.

"Johnson has made a slip of the pen, and written Philips instead of Richardson, who, says p. xcix, that his third wife was, he had heard, a 'termagant;' but Richardson is silent on the subject of the oppression and the cheating" (Cunningham). It has been conjectured that Richardson's informant was Deborah Milton, the youngest daughter.

l. 28, **cheated them at his death.** Milton left all his money

to his third wife, by a "nuncupative will," that is, a purely
verbal statement of his desire as to the disposal of his property,
made by a dying man before witnesses, and afterwards put in
writing by them. Disputes over such wills (now only valid in
the case of soldiers and sailors on active service) were frequent,
and they were always looked on with suspicion. A lawsuit was
threatened by the disinherited daughters, and the will, which
has since been found by Thomas Warton, and printed in 1791,
after Johnson's death, was not insisted upon ; but by a com-
promise the widow took two-thirds of the estate, while the rest
was divided between the three daughters. See Cunningham's
edition of the " Lives of the Poets," i. 166-8.

This is the foundation for the charge that Milton's third wife
" cheated " his children after their father's death. The deposi-
tions made by the poet's brother, Christopher (who drew up and
wrote the will himself after hearing the dying man's wishes),
and by others, entirely clear her. Compare p. 50, l. 7.

l. 30, **according to an obscure story.** This is given in
Richardson's " Life " (page c), on the authority of Henry
Bendish (a descendant of the Lord Protector), who had heard
Milton's " widow or daughter, or both, say it." The story is
probably without any basis of truth.

l. 31, **his employment,** viz., the Latin Secretaryship.

p. 34, l. 9, **the new settlement.** The Restoration Government.

l. 13, **" Accidence commenced Grammar."** This is a first
Latin book. Accidence was that part of grammar which taught
the inflexions of words, and was formerly learned before the
more scientific study of grammar was begun. In his preface
Milton complains that the " tenth part of a man's life ordinarily
extended is taken up in learning, and that very scarcely, the
Latin tongue. Which tardy proficience may be attributed to
several causes : in particular, the making two labours of one, by
learning first the Accidence, then the Grammar in Latin, ere
the language of those rules be understood. The only remedy
was to join both books into one, and in the English tongue."
" Accidence commenced grammar " means " Accidence taking a
higher place as grammar."   Cf. p. 108.

Johnson's date, taken from Antony Wood, seems to be wrong.
The book was apparently published in 1669, at least no edition
of an earlier date has been found. It is printed in the Bohn
edition, v. 432-479.

l. 20, **Elwood the Quaker.** Thomas Ellwood (1639-1718)
has left us a charming autobiography, for a cheap issue of which
we have to thank Professor Henry Morley and Messrs. Rout-
ledge. He was a simple and beautiful-minded young man, who

had joined the Quakers about a couple of years, when he was
introduced to Milton, whom he describes as " a gentleman of
great note for learning throughout the learned world, for the
accurate pieces he had written on various subjects and occasions," by Dr. Paget, already mentioned as Milton's medical
attendant and friend. (" History of Thomas Ellwood," Morley's
Universal Library, pp. 132-8, cf. pp. 184, 186, *et passim*).

l. 23, letter to Hartlib. " Of Education. To Master S.
Hartlib " (Milton's " Prose Works," Bohn, iii. 462-478). Johnson's quotation will be found on p. 468.

Samuel Hartlib (died after 1662) was of Polish extraction; he
came to England in 1628, and devoted himself and his fortune
to experiments in education and agriculture. He received a
pension from Cromwell. He wrote several works on agriculture,
and Sir William Petty addressed to him two or three of his
pamphlets.

l. 25, Law French. A very corrupt form of Norman French
used by the mediæval lawyers.

l. 27, he said. "·At my first sitting to read to him, observing
that I used the English pronunciation, he told me, if I would
have the benefit of the Latin tongue, not only to read and understand Latin authors, but to converse with foreigners, either
abroad or at home, I must learn the foreign pronunciation. To
this I consenting, he instructed me how to sound the vowels ;
so different from the common pronunciation used by the English, who speak Anglice their Latin, that—with some few other
variations in sounding some consonants in particular cases, as
c before *e* or *i* like *ch*, *sc* before *i* like *sh*, etc.—the Latin thus
spoken seemed as different from that which was delivered as
the English generally speak it, as if it were another language "
(Ellwood, pp. 184-5).

p. 35, l. 3, for he relates. Ellwood, p. 136.

l. 7, Artillery Walk. This has now disappeared, and its
place is taken by Bunhill Row. It was a road running by the
side of the Artillery Ground, where the City Trained Bands
used to exercise, not half a mile from Milton's previous residences
in Barbican and Jewin Street.

Bunhill Fields, an open space continuous with the Artillery
Ground, set aside as a burial ground by the City of London,
contains the ashes of many famous Nonconformists, amongst
them Bunyan, Defoe, and Dr. Watts.

l. 11, He was now busied. According to Aubrey, who got
his information from Philips, Milton had begun the epic of
"Paradise Lost " in 1658. It was finished in the summer of 1665.

l. 15, in an Italian tragedy. The "Adamo" of Andreini,
called " a farce " in the next line.

l. 16, **a farce seen by Milton.** This was the sacred play, "Adamo," by Andreini, an Italian poet (1578-1660), published in 1613. The drama, which consists of five acts, with songs and choruses, is not nearly so absurd as Voltaire (" Œuvres," viii. 553) pretends, and it has been translated by Cowper. See Southey's edition of " Cowper," x. 239-387.

That Milton did owe something to Andreini is now generally acknowledged. Other possible or probable sources of suggestion are Caedmon, Grotius (" Adamus Exul") and Vondel (" Lucifer"). See Masson, Globe edit., pp. 9-10.

l. 17, **It has already been shown.** See p. 26 above.

l. 24, **He long before had promised.** In the Introduction to Book II. of the " Reason of Church Government urged against Prelaty " (1641) (Bohn, ii. 472-482). This piece of lofty and dignified egotism contains some of Milton's finest prose.

l. 29, **it was difficult to determine.** Among the Milton manuscripts preserved in Trinity College Library, Cambridge, these jottings of "no fewer than ninety-nine possible themes—sixty-one scriptural and thirty-eight historical or legendary. Four of these relate to ' Paradise Lost.' Among the most remarkable of the other subjects are ' Sodom ' (the plan is detailed at considerable length, and, though evidently impractical, is interesting as a counterpart of ' Comus '), ' Samson Marrying,' ' Ahab,' ' John the Baptist,' ' Christus Patiens,' ' Vortigern,' ' Alfred the Great,' ' Athirco ' (a very striking subject from a Scotch legend), and ' Macbeth,' where Duncan's ghost was to have appeared instead of Banquo's, and seemingly take a share in the action. ' Arthur,' so much in his mind when he wrote the ' Epitaphium Damonis,' does not appear at all " (Dr. Garnett, " Life of Milton," pp. 129-130).

He was long chusing. See note to p. 25, l. 33.

l. 35, **episodes.** Incidents not directly advancing the main story, but introduced to enliven it. A technical word with critics.

accumulate images and sentiments, lay up in his mind similes or comparisons, and judgments, on men and things. " Sentiment" is no longer commonly used in this sense of opinion or judgment.

p. 36, l. 4, **a statesman,** an official of the state.

l. 9, **by Mr. Richardson.** See note to p. 32, l. 11. See Richardson, " Explanatory Notes to ' Paradise Lost,' " p. iv.

l. 13, **of distinguished parts as well as quality,** of distinguished abilities as well as of high social position. Such were Marvell, Aubrey, Davenant, Dryden, Lady Ranelagh, the Earl of Anglesey (see p. 45). Aubrey says (p. 388) that Milton was "visited much by learned [sc. persons] more than he did desire."

Toland says that the Earl of Anglesey, " as well as several of
the nobility and gentry, was his constant visitor " (" Life,"
Milton's " Prose Works," 1698, p. 43).

l. 19, **Another account.** This other picture of Milton was
given Richardson by " an ancient clergyman in Dorsetshire,
Dr. Wright." See Richardson's " Explanatory Notes," p. iv.
" He found him in a small house, he thinks but one room
on a floor ; in that, up one pair of stairs, which was hung with
a rusty green, he found John Milton."

l. 22, **chalkstones.** A fine white substance resembling
chalk, sometimes secreted by the skin of the hands and feet of
gouty persons.

l. 25, **to swing in a chair.** " After he was blind he used to
swing for exercise " (Richardson, p. v). Toland tells us that
" he had a pulley to swing and keep him in motion " (" Life,"
Milton's " Prose Works," 1698, p. 46).

l. 34, **Mr. Philips observes.** " Life of Milton," Godwin,
p. 376. " Philips told the same story to Aubrey " (Cunningham).
See Godwin, pp. 343-44 for this.

l. 35, **composure.** This sense of the word is obsolete. We
should say, composition.

p. 37, l. 4, **parcels,** small parts. Fr. *parcelle,* from Lat.
particula, the diminutive of *pars,* a part.

l. 9, **his vein,** his imagination, fancy. Cf.—

> " Nothing that's plain
> But may be witty, if thou hast the vein " (Herbert).

l, 10, **from the Autumnal Equinox to the Vernal.** Compare
Cowper—" When I can find no other occupation, I think ; and
when I think, I am very apt to do it in rhyme. Hence it comes
to pass that the season of the year which generally pinches off
the flowers of poetry, unfolds mine, such as they are, and
crowns me with a winter garland " (Letter to Joseph Hill,
May 9th, 1781).

l. 15, **Toland remarks.** " Life of Milton," p. 127. Richardson
gives Toland's opinion, and discusses the whole question,
pp. cxiii. *seq.*

l. 17, **his Elegies.** " Elegia Quinta," v. 5-6.

> " Fallor ? An et nobis redeunt in carmina vires
> Ingeniumque mihi munere veris adest ? "

This elegy was written at the age of twenty, hence the force of
Johnson's remark, ll. 20-22.

l. 22, **Mr. Richardson conceives.** " Explanatory Notes,"
p. cxiv.

l. 31, **Sapiens dominabitur astris.** "'The wise man will be master of the constellations;' a saying ascribed to one of the Ptolemies; an allusion to the astrological beliefs in the influence of the planets upon a man's life and actions" (Professor Deighton's note).

l. 32, **weather-bound,** prevented by the weather from doing anything.

l. 33, **hellebore.** Hellebore is an ambiguous name given to two distinct kinds of plants. Black Hellebore, or Christmas Rose, and White Hellebore (*Veratrum album*). Both are poisonous, the latter especially so; both have been largely employed in medicine, especially in cases of mania and melancholia. Compare Burton's "Anatomy of Melancholy," Part 2, Sect. 4, Mem. 2, Subsec. 1, 2.

p. 38, l. 1, **possunt quia.** "Æneid," v. 231.

l. 9, **world was in its decay.** Sir John Hawkins says that Dr. Gabriel Goodman, Bishop of Gloucester, first put forward this opinion in this country, in a book called "The Fall of Man, or the Corruption of Nature proved by Natural Reason" (1616). The opinion, however, was common enough. See, for instance, Sir Thomas Browne, "Urn Burial," cap. v., "We whose generations are ordained in this setting part of time," etc.

l. 16, **an age too late.** Matthew Arnold, in his edition of Johnson's "Lives," loosely refers to "The Reason of Church Government" urged against Prelaty;" and Mrs. Napier and Professor Deighton follow him. The quotation, however, occurs in the well-known passage at the beginning of Book IX. of "Paradise Lost:"

> "Me, of these
> Nor skilled nor studious, higher argument
> Remains, sufficient of itself to raise
> That name, unless an age too late, or cold
> Climate, or years, damp my intended wing
> Depressed."   (vv. 41-46.)

With this may be compared the passage which Matthew Arnold probably had in his mind in the "Reason of Church Government," Book II., Introduction, Bohn, ii. 478-79. "And as Tasso gave to a prince of Italy his choice whether he would command him to write of Godfrey's expedition against the Infidels, or Belisarius against the Goths, or Charlemaine against the Lombards: if to the instinct of nature and the emboldening of art aught may be trusted, and *that there be nothing adverse in our climate or the fate of our age*, it haply would be no rashness, from an equal diligence and inclination, to present the like offer in our ancient stories."

Professor Deighton quotes from Macaulay's "Essay on Milton:" "He doubted, as he has himself owned, whether he had not been born ' an age too late.' For this notion Johnson has thought fit to make him the butt of much clumsy ridicule. The poet, we believe, understood the nature of his art better than the critic. He knew that his poetical genius derived no advantage from the civilization which surrounded him, or from the learning which he had acquired : and he looked back with something like regret to the ruder age of simple words and vivid impressions" ("Essays," Student's Edition, pp. 2-8).

Macaulay, however, in this passage, goes beyond Milton, who thought that for the education of the poet, there "must be added industrious and select reading, steady observation, insight into all seemly and generous arts and affairs" (Bohn, ii. 481).

p. 39, l. 2, **frosty grovellers,** men of chilled minds obliged to grope on the ground.

l. 4, **they should not willingly let die.** "Reason of Church Government," Introduction to Book II., Bohn, ii. 478.

l. 7, **the dwindle.** Used as a substantive. Johnson does not mention this use in his "Dictionary ; " and the only authority cited by Hunter ("Encyclopedic Dict.") and Whitney (" Century Dict.") is this passage.

l. 8, **giant of the pygmies.** The pygmies were dwarfs mentioned by (Homer "Iliad," iii. 5). They got their name from πυγμή, a measure of 18½ inches. By "giant of the pygmies" Johnson probably means a reference to Gulliver among the Lilliputians.

l. 8, **one-eyed monarch of the blind.** "Among the blind the one-eyed is king."

l. 14, **relates that.** Richardson, "Explanatory Notes," p. cxiv.

l. 17, **œstrum.** This should be œstrus, which means, a wasp, or gadfly. By transference of meaning it signifies frenzy, or inspiration. The word is used by Richardson in the above-mentioned passage.

l. 84, **never taught to write.** This is only true of Anne, the eldest. Both the others could write. They were badly educated, however.

p. 40, l. 8, **reducing his exuberance,** by compressing, and by striking out bad lines. The same thing is told of Virgil.

l. 11, **unpremeditated verse.** "Paradise Lost," ix. 24.

l. 22, **cleared from all effects of his disloyalty.** No longer amenable to law in consequence of his disloyalty.

l. 28, **fallen on evil days.** "Paradise Lost," vii. 23-28.

p. 41, l. 2, **he never spared any asperity of reproach.** Compare Introduction, p. xxvii., on the style; and p. 95 above, on the substance of this remark.

Mark Pattison speaks of Milton's prose pamphlets in perfectly just terms. "He is a zealot among the zealots; his cause is the cause of God; and the sword of the Independents is the sword of the Lord and of Gideon. He does not refute opponents, but curses enemies. Yet his rage, even when most delirious, is always a Miltonic rage; it is grand, sublime, terrible! Mingled with the scurrilities of the theological brawl are passages of the noblest English ever written. . . . Milton's capacity of emotion when once he became champion of a cause could not be contained within the bounds of ordinary speech. It breaks into ferocious reprobation, into terrific blasts of vituperation, beneath which the very language creaks, as the timbers of a ship in a storm" ("Milton," p. 65-66).

l. 10, **the wit**, the man of intelligence and originality. Johnson defines a wit, in this sense as "a man of fancy; a man of genius."

l. 13, **Chalfont.** This is Chalfont St. Giles, four miles from Amersham, and about as far from Rickmansworth. The "pretty box" which Ellwood took for Milton still stands.

Elwood. See p. 117. Ellwood relates this in his Autobiography, pp. 199-200.

l. 20, **A license was necessary.** The officials charged with the duty of licensing new books "in divinity, physic, philosophy, poetry, or whatsoever," were Archbishop of Canterbury, the Bishop of London, or some persons appointed by them (usually their chaplains), and the chancellors or vice-chancellors of the universities. The licenser of "Paradise Lost" was the Rev. Thomas Tomkyns, chaplain to Dr. Sheldon, Archbishop of Canterbury.

l. 24, **the simile of the sun eclipsed.** "Paradise Lost," i. 594-599. The vagaries of licensers are always difficult to understand. According to the story, the worthy Mr. Tomkyns seems to have seen a possible kind of disloyalty in the suggestion that "monarchs" could be "perplexed with fear of change." But he did not insist on suppressing the poem, or even cutting out the incriminated passage.

The story, which rests on very slight foundations, comes from Toland's "Life," prefixed to the 1698 edition of Milton's "Prose Works," pp. 40-41. No authority is mentioned. "I must not forget that we had like to be eternally deprived of this treasure by the ignorance or malice of the licenser, who, among other frivolous exceptions, would needs suppress the whole poem for imaginary treason in the following lines:

'As when the sun new risen
Looks through the horizontal misty air

Shorn of his beams, or from behind the moon
In dim eclipse disastrous twilight sheds
On half the nations, and with fear of change
Perplexes monarchs.' "

l. 26, **his copy.** Technical term for manuscript handed to the printer.

Samuel Simmons. His shop was "next door to the Golden Lion in Aldersgate Street."

"The original of this famous agreement [that is, the copy which Simmons retained] is in the British Museum, having been presented to that institution in 1852 by Samuel Rogers, the poet, who had purchased it in 1831 for a hundred guineas from Mr. Pickering, the publisher. It had come down in the possession of the famous publishing family, the Tonsons. The signature, however, is not actually in Milton's own handwriting" (Mrs. Napier's note). A facsimile is given in Masson's "Life of Milton," vi. 511. The first book of Milton's MS. submitted to the licenser, with the *imprimatur*, has been also preserved by the Tonsons.

The particulars of the arrangement with Simmons will be found in the Globe edition, pp. 2-8.

l. 34, **quarto.** A book printed on sheets folded twice, so that the page is half the size of a folio printed on the same kind of paper. See p. 111, above.

the titles, the title-pages. This is still the technical term. The different title-pages (of which there were nine) are given by Mr. Masson in the Globe edition, pp. 3-4.

p. 42, l. 6, **octavo.** A book printed on sheets folded four times, so that the page is half the size of a quarto printed on the same kind of paper.

l. 8, **other small improvements.** "Arguments" were prefixed to the books, or rather the long Argument prefixed to the later issues of the first edition, was split up and placed at the beginning of the several books. (See Globe edition, p. 4.)

l. 13, **Brabazon Aylmer.** Another bookseller, whose shop was in Cornhill. He published, in 1674, Milton's Latin letters, with some of the Latin college exercises. See p. 47 above.

l. 14, **Jacob Tonson.** This famous bookseller (1656-1736), was the founder of modern publishing. He set the example of dealing more liberally with authors than had been the custom of the trade. He published for Otway and Dryden, Tate and Rowe, as well as for Addison and Pope on their first appearance. At his house at Barn Elms, near Putney, he used to entertain the members of the famous Kit-Cat Club. Several members of the family became partners of "old Jacob," and he was succeeded as head of the firm by a grandnephew, Jacob Tonson the third (died 1767), of whom Johnson speaks as "a man who is to be praised as often as he is named." (See below, p. 54, l. 11.)

l. 16, **a deduction**, an account which traces events step by step. An unusual sense of the word.

l. 26, **no publick acclamations** That it was not an unpopular book is, however, shown by what Johnson says on p. 48. Six editions were sold in the seventeenth century, three of them (1688,1692, 1695), large and expensive folios. The edition of 1688 has a list of over 500 subscribers, including the names of many of the most notable persons of the day.

Three more (1705, 1707, 1711) followed before Addison's famous papers on "Paradise Lost" appeared in the "Spectator" (1712).

p. 43, l. 6, **a closet of knowledge**, a cupboard of books, a small library.

l. 19, **new to all and disgusting to many.** Blank verse was of course not really new, since it had been always employed for dramatic purposes until the Restoration, and there were a few instances of its employment in non-dramatic pieces. It had, however, entirely gone out of fashion since the adoption of the heroic couplet. See Milton's prefatory remark on "the Verse" prefixed to the "Paradise Lost."

disgusting, distasteful. Johnson uses it in a much milder sense than ourselves. Cf. p. 56, l. 6, above.

l. 20, **the prevalence of genius**, the prevailing power possessed by genius.

l. 24, **did not dare to publish their opinion.** This is not true. In 1674, directly after Milton's death, Dryden (a wit and a member of the court party) spoke of the "Paradise Lost" "as undoubtedly one of the greatest, most noble and most sublime poems which either this age or nation has produced" (Preface to "The State of Innocence."). His generous, if uncritical, lines prefixed to the folio of 1688, are well known :

> "Three poets in three distant ages born,
> Greece, Italy, and England did adorn,
> The first in loftiness of mind surpassed,
> The next in majesty, in both the last;
> The force of Nature could no further go,
> To make the third she joined the other two."

In his "Discourse on Satire" (prefixed to the translation of Juvenal and Persius, 1692), Dryden speaks of Milton as an established favourite, "Mr. Milton, whom we all admire with so much justice." Translations were made into German (1682), and Latin (1686).

l. 30, **price of the copy.** The value of the right of publishing the copy (see note to p. 41, l. 26) continually advanced.

p. 44, l. 10, **Mr. Philips tells us.** " Life of Milton," Godwin, p. 380-381.

l. 13, **as well reap . . . as oblige.** Both reap . . . and oblige ; not only oblige . . . but also reap. . . . This usage is obsolete.

l. 17, **her bodily infirmity.** Anne Milton was lame.

l. 19, **I doubt,** I suspect.

l. 26, **confined,** obliged.

l. 31, **curious,** excellent, rare.

l. 32, **proper,** suitable.

p. 45, l. 8, **"History of England."** See p. 25. "The History of Britain " was published in 1670, though written for the most part long before. The first four books were written before he became Latin secretary, the remaining two during the Commonwealth. Milton's " Prose Works," Bohn, v. 164-393.

l. 9, **Geoffry of Monmouth.** Geoffrey of Monmouth, a monk of the twelfth century, who became Archdeacon of Monmouth, and (in 1152) Bishop of St. Asaph. His " Historia Regum Britanniæ," written by the year 1147, professes to be a translation of an authentic Welsh original, but is undoubtedly in the main a compilation of legends and scraps from previous chroniclers, woven together by a free use of the constructive imagination. The fabulous character of his work was very early recognized. Thus, forty years later, Giraldus Cambrensis, in his " Itinerarium," tells a story of a man haunted by the sight of devils, which vanished when the Gospels were put on his breast, but which when Geoffrey's book was placed there " reappeared in great numbers, and remained a longer time than usual on his body and on the book." In Geoffrey's chronicle first appear the stories of Lear, Cymbeline, Merlin, and Arthur. The Arthur legend was first put into systematic form by this important writer.

l. 16, **the licenser again fixed his claws.** Compare pp. 41 and 123. Toland is the authority for this story also. " Life," Milton's " Prose Works," 1698, p. 43.

l. 21, **earl of Anglesea.** Arthur Annesley, second Viscount Valentia and Earl of Anglesey (1614-86), was President of the Council of State after Cromwell's death, and helped to bring about the Restoration. He was one of Milton's friends and visitors, according to Toland.

l, 22, **since been inserted.** " Prose Works," Bohn, v. 236-41. The passage is on the failure of the Puritan revolution, " the ill-husbanding of those fair opportunities which might seem to have put liberty, so long desired, like a bridle into their hands." It was first inserted in the 1738 edition of Milton's prose works, which contains the life by Dr. Birch.

l. 23, **"Paradise Regained."** This and the "Samson Agonistes" were issued in one volume in 1671, or perhaps the latter part of 1670. The volume was licensed in July, 1670, by Tomkyns, who had licensed the "Paradise Lost."

l. 26, **another bookseller.** John Starkey, at the Mitre in Fleet Street, near Temple Bar. It was, however, apparently published by Starkey at the author's own risk. See Masson, Globe edit., p. 284.

l. 34, **to Elwood.** "History of Thomas Ellwood," p. 200.

p. 46, l. 4, **as Elwood relates.** This is a mistake; no such remark occurs in Ellwood's autobiography. It is doubtless a slip of the pen for Philips. "It ['Paradise Regained'] is generally censured to be much inferior to the other, though he could not hear with patience any such thing when related to him." Godwin, "Lives," p. 379. There is not sufficient ground here for Johnson to say that "Paradise Regained" was Milton's favourite. Compare Mark Pattison, "Milton," pp. 192, *seq.*

l. 18, **did not disdain the meanest services.** Compare Wordsworth's sonnet on Milton:

> " Thy soul was like a star, and dwelt apart :
> Thou hadst a voice whose sound was like the sea,
> Pure as the naked Heavens, majestic, free ;
> So didst thou travel on life's common way
> In cheerful godliness ; and yet thy heart
> The lowliest duties on herself did lay."

l. 25, **Ramus.** Petrus Ramus (Pierre de la Ramée) (1515-71), a French scholar and thinker, one of the anti-scholastic teachers of philosophy. Notwithstanding his attacks on the Aristotelian logic, he was made Professor of Philosophy at the Collége Royal. Towards the close of his life he became a Protestant, and perished in the massacre of St. Bartholomew. The substantive changes in logic suggested by Ramus were very slight; the influence of the "Ramists" was mainly critical and destructive. See Hallam, "History of European Literature," i. 394-97.

Professor Masson thinks that both the "Logic" and the "Accidence" of Milton were mainly the work of his life at Cambridge, put into shape and published long afterwards. "Life of Milton," i. 264 ; vi. 685.

l. 32, **"Treatise of True Religion."** Published in 1673,

with no printer's or publisher's name. Milton's "Prose Works,"
Bohn, ii. 509-19.

p. 47, l. 7, **we have no warrant.** "Treatise of True Religion,"
Bohn, ii. 515.

It has been usually forgotten that Milton's toleration was of
a very limited kind. He was willing to tolerate people who
differed very slightly from himself; but Roman Catholics and
"Prelatists" (what we should now call High Churchmen) he
would suppress by force. Sir Thomas More, in his "Utopia,"
and Jeremy Taylor, in his "Liberty of Prophesying," not to
speak of John Hales and Grotius, had set him an example of
much greater breadth of toleration.

Milton left behind him a Latin theological treatise, which was
not published till 1825, when it served as a text for Macaulay's
famous essay on Milton. This is a long and elaborate treatise,
"De Doctrina Christiana, ex sacris duntaxat libris petita,"
which was discovered in the old State Paper Office at Whitehall in 1823. It was translated by Dr. Charles Sumner, afterwards Bishop of Winchester, and the translation is inserted in
the Bohn edition of Milton's "Prose Works," vols. iv.-v.

l. 12, **one of the Pope's bulls.** Bohn, ii. 510.

l. 16, **perusal of the Scriptures.** Bohn, ii. 517.

l. 18, **He now reprinted.** "Poems of Mr. John Milton upon
several occasions, both English and Latin. With a small Tractate
of Education to Mr. Hartlib" (1673), 8vo.

The additions comprise the "Ode on the Death of a Fair
Infant," "At a Vacation Exercise," "On the New Forcers of
Conscience," nine new sonnets (xi., xii., xiii., xiv., xviii., xix.,
xx., xxi., xxiii.), and some Psalms.

l. 21, **"Familiar Epistles."** "Joannis Miltonii Angli Epistolarum familiarium liber unus, quibus accesserunt ejusdem jam
olim in collegio adolescentis prolersiones quædam oratoriæ"
(1674), 12mo. A translation will be found in Milton's "Prose
Works," Bohn, iii. 487-522. There are thirty-one letters, none
of any particular interest.

On the "Prolusiones Academicæ," see Masson, "Life of
Milton," i. 239-275, ed. 1859.

l. 30, **expiration,** death. The word is no longer used in this
sense.

Milton died on November 8, 1674, being sixty-six years old, all
but one month.

l. 31, **in Bunhill-fields,** i.e., in Artillery Walk.

next his father. His father died in 1647, see p. 103.

l. 34 **supposed to have been no monument.** Aubrey says the
stone that covered Milton's grave " is now removed; for about
two years since (now 1681) the two steps to the communion

table were raised.   I guess, John Speed and he lie together "
(Aubrey's " Life of Milton," in Godwin's " Lives," p. 346).

No monument seems to have been erected until 1793, when
Mr. Samuel Whitbread placed a marble bust in the church.
Fenton speaks of a small monument of which the inscription
had long been illegible; but Bishop Newton, in his "Life of
Milton" prefixed to his edition of the "Paradise Lost," shows
that Fenton must have been misinformed.

In 1790, under the site of the old chancel of St. Giles', a coffin
was found which was believed to be that of Milton, and a shameful mutilation of the remains took place.   There seems, however,
good reason to hope that the relic-snatchers had hit on a wrong
coffin, and that the dust of the great poet lies undisturbed.
See John Ashton, "Eighteenth Century Waifs," pp. 55 seq.

p. 48, l. 2, **Mr. Benson.** This was William Benson, Surveyor
of Buildings to George I.   On the monument (the portrait bust
is by Rysbrach the famous sculptor) he placed an inscription of
several lines, in which nothing is said about Milton, while the
fact that the bust was erected by " William Benson, Esq., one
of the two Auditors of the imprests to his Majesty King George
II., formerly Surveyor-General of the Works to his Majesty
King George I.," is duly recorded.   "On poet's tombs see
Benson's titles writ," says Pope (" Dunciad," iii. 325), while in
a note, not at all complimentary, he remarks : "In favour
of this man the famous Sir Christopher Wren, who had been
Architect to the Crown for above fifty years, who built most of
the churches in London, . . . had been displaced from his employment at the age of near ninety years."

l. 4, **Philips.** This is not Milton's nephew, but John Philips
(1676-1708), the author of "The Splendid Shilling" and
"Cyder."   See Johnson's "Lives of the Poets," Bohn, i.
325-341.

l. 6, **Dr. Sprat.** Thomas Sprat (1636-1713), Dean of Westminster (1683), and Bishop of Rochester (1684), a Tory wit and
divine, and one of the very inferior writers who make their
appearance in Johnson's " Lives of the Poets." See Bohn, ii.
41-47.

l. 9, **Atterbury.** Francis Atterbury (1662-1732), another
famous Tory wit, who was made Dean of Westminster and
Bishop of Rochester in 1713.   He was one of the friends of
Pope, Swift, and Bolingbroke, and died in exile, banished for
life by the Whigs, not after a trial before a jury, but by a bill
of pains and penalties.

l. 11, **said Dr. Gregory.** "This was no doubt David Gregory,
D.D. (1696-1767), who, when Johnson went up to Oxford,
in 1728, was Professor of Modern History and Languages,

George I. having founded that Chair in 1728. When Johnson
visited Oxford in 1759, Gregory had then been for three years
Dean of Christchurch" (Mrs. Napier's note).

l. 13, **a statue.** The monument takes the form of a bust, and
not of a statue.

l. 16, **the Lady of his college.** Aubrey, Godwin, p. 337.

l. 17, **light brown.** "He had light brown hair. His complexion exceeding fair. (He was so fair they called him the
Lady of Christ's College.) Oval face, his eyes a dark grey"
(Aubrey, Godwin, p. 337). Richardson says that Milton's eyes
were "inclined to blue, not deep" (p. iii).

"He was of fair complexion, a little red in his cheeks, and
light brown hair" (George Vertue's letter in "Gentleman's
Magazine," 1776, p. 200; on the authority of Deborah Clarke,
Milton's daughter).

l. 18, **the foretop,** the middle. See his portraits.

l. 19, **he has given of Adam.** "Paradise Lost," iv. 301-303:

" Hyacinthine locks
Round from his parted forelock manly hung
Clustering, but not beneath his shoulders broad."

l. 21, **according to Mr. Richardson.** "Life," p. ii. Aubrey
says, "he was scarce so tall as I am," and explains that he himself is "of middle stature." He adds that "Milton was a spare
man," which is somewhat in contradiction to the statement of
Richardson given by Johnson. (Godwin, p. 337.)

l. 23, **exercise of the sword.** "When he was young he
learned to fence, probably as a gentlemanly accomplishment"
(Richardson, p. v). "His recreations before his sight was gone
consisted much in feats of activity, particularly in the exercise of
his arms which he could handle with activity" (Toland, p. 46).

l. 26, **backsword,** a sword having a sharp edge and a back,
capable of striking, whereas the rapier has no edge and is used
only for thrusting. Milton does not mention the "backsword"
in his tract "On Education," but clearly implies it. "The exercise which I commend first, is the exact use of their weapon, to
guard and to strike safely with edge or point" (Bohn, iii. 475).

l. 28, **never to have been bright.** The authority for this has
escaped me.

l. 31, **little strong drink.** Aubrey, Toland, and Richardson
all mention this.

l. 34, **studied late at night.** Toland, p. 46; Aubrey, Godwin,
p. 339.

p. 49, l. 1, **The course of his day.** "He was an early riser,
sc. at 4 o'clock mane, yea, after he lost his sight. He had a man
read to him. The first thing he read was the Hebrew Bible.

NOTES, PAGES 48-50.   131

. . . then he contemplated. At 7 his man came to him again,
and then read to him and wrote till dinner. The writing was as
much as the reading. . . . After dinner he used to walk three
or four hours at a time (he always had a garden where he
lived) ; went to bed about nine." Milton had " a delicate, tune-
able voice and had good skill . . . His father instructed him.
He had an organ in his house and played on that most "
(Aubrey, Godwin, p. 388).

l. 9, **even tenour**, the regular course of his life. Tenour, or
tenor, comes from French, *teneur*—Latin, *tenor -em*, that which
holds on, the general course. In old music the melody was
usually given to the highest men's voices, which held the tune
while the other voices, above and below, added harmonies.

l. 11, **succession of his practice**, the regular order of events
in his daily life.

l. 16, **something read to him by his bedside**. Toland, p. 46.

l. 17, **were employed**, *sc.* in their household duties, or other
daily tasks. (Cf. p. 44).

l. 20, **his leg thrown over the arm**. Richardson, p. cxiv.

l. 21, **Fortune**, wealth, money.

l. 22, **lent his personal estate**. Personal estate means
property other than land or houses.

l. 28, **two hundred pounds a year**. His salary was nearly
three hundred, viz., £288 a year. When his growing blindness
obliged him to have an assistant it was reduced to £150.

l. 29, **had a thousand pounds**. This is a mistake. See note
to p. 21, l. 4.

l. 30, **Namptwich**, now called Nantwich.

l. 31, **about 1729**. Probably in September, 1727, at the age
of eighty-nine.

l. 32, **by entrusting it to a scrivener**. On scrivener, see
p. 82.

l. 34, **grasped an estate**. He bought an estate belonging to
the Chapter of Westminster, when the estates of the Abbey were
sold by order of Parliament.

p. 50, l. 3, **placed in the Excise-office**. The money had been
lent by Milton to the Commissioners of Excise in the time of
the Commonwealth. "He sustained such losses as might well
have broke any person less frugal and temperate than himself;
no less than £2,000 which he had put for security and improvement into the Excise Office, but neglecting to recall it in time,
could never after get it out, with all the power and interest he
had in the great ones of those times; besides another great sum,
by mismanagement and for want of good advice" (Philips,
Godwin, p. 382).

l. 4, **reduced to indigence**. Even after the Restoration

Milton was in comfortable circumstances. "On the whole, Milton appears to have saved about £1,500 from the wreck of his fortunes, and to have possessed about £200 income from this interest of this fund and other sources, destined to be yet further reduced within a few years" (Dr. Garnett, "Life of Milton," p. 141). Milton's two hundred a year would be worth about seven hundred a year nowadays. On Milton's pecuniary circumstances after the Restoration, see Masson, vi. 444, *seq.*

l. 6, **sold his library.** Toland, pp. 45-46.

l. 7, **on which his widow laid hold.** See p. 88, l. 28, and pp. 116-117.

Johnson's figures are not quite correct. Milton left not £1,500 besides household goods, as Philips had heard and as Toland repeated, but about £1,000. See Masson, "Life," vi. 743-744.

l. 9, **his literature,** his learning, knowledge of books.

l. 11, **polite,** polished. "Polite learning" means what is now called *belles lettres,* viz., poetry, fiction, and essays, where the manner is more important than the matter. By a "polite language" Johnson means one in which such literature has been written. To the Englishmen of the eighteenth century Hebrew was a learned language, and Italian a polite language; while Latin and Greek came under both heads.

its two dialects, viz., Hebrew proper and Aramaic, another closely-allied Semitic language, one form of which (Syriac) was spoken almost universally in Palestine at the time of Christ. Certain parts of the Bible are written in another dialect of Aramaic (*e.g.,* part of Daniel and Ezra), and our Lord frequently quotes the Aramaic version of the purely Hebrew scriptures.

l. 15, **his daughter.** Mrs. Clarke. See p. 58.

l. 17, **Ovid's "Metamorphoses."** Publius Ovidius Naso (43 B.C.-9 A.D.), the famous Roman poet, wrote his "Metamorphoses" about the opening of the Christian era. The poem consists of fifteen books of stories of legendary transformations, without much connection.

l. 18, **Euripides.** Euripides, the third of the great tragic poets of Greece (480-406 B.C.), a friend of Socrates. Amongst other plays, he wrote "Alcestis," "Electra," and "Orestes." In her "Wine of Cyprus" Mrs. Browning thus characterizes him:

> "Our Euripides the human,
>   With his droppings of warm tears,
> And his touches of things common,
>   Till they rose to touch the spheres!"

l. 18, **Mr. Cradock.** This was a Leicestershire gentleman, who wrote a tragedy called "Zobeide" and some "Memoirs of his Own Times." See Boswell, "Life of Johnson," Bohn, iii. 86-7.

l. 30, **Calvinistical.** John Calvin (1509-1564), the most logical as well as the most pious of the early reformers, systematized the Protestant theology in his "Christianæ Religionis Institutio," and taught doctrines which denied human Free-will and practically made God the author of sin. God predestines the "elect" to eternal happiness, and others to eternal damnation. Calvin established a kind of theocratic government at Geneva, which served as a model for other Presbyterian churches. He greatly influenced the Protestant party in the Church of England ; and some of the Articles of the Church of England were drawn in a Calvinistic sense.

l. 31, **Arminianism.** Arminius (the Latinized form of Harmensen) was the name of a famous Dutch Protestant divine (died 1609), who, in opposition to the current Calvinism, taught that God does not eternally predestine those who are not "elect " to eternal damnation. The orthodox Calvinists nicknamed all who took this view " Arminians," and the opposition of the Puritans to Laud and his party was perhaps even more due to their "Arminianism " than to their supposed Romanizing tendencies. Milton's treatise, "De Doctrinâ Christianâ," rejects the doctrine of "reprobation " of the wicked by eternal decree of God. See Bohn, iv. 64.

l. 34, **Baudius.** Dominic Baudius (died 1613), a scholar and Latin poet, who was at one time professor of history at Leyden. "This saying of his is quoted by Jortin in his ' Life of Erasmus,' vol. ii., p. 7, ed. 1760 " (Mrs. Napier's note). Johnson's next sentence gives the sense of the Latin quotation.

p. 51 l. 15, **untainted by any heretical peculiarity.** Although the terms "Trinity," "Triune," etc., are not used in the "Paradise Lost," even so acute a theologian as Cardinal Newman did not consider the poem as unorthodox. But before he died Milton had definitely adopted unorthodox opinions as to the divinity of Christ, and avows them in his Latin " Treatise on Christian Doctrine," first published in 1825.

l. 17, **immediate and occasional agency,** the direct interference of God in human affairs on special occasions.

l. 18, **without any visible worship.** Toland, p. 46.

l. 21, **acceptably.** Because still free from sin.

l. 24, **with their own approbation.** Johnson means the doctrine that each man's conscience is his own sufficient guide in matters of this kind, that as long as a man is satisfied with his own conduct in matters of religion no further demand can be made on him.

l. 27, **efficaciously.** Their prayers were received and answered,

after the Fall, because presented by "their great Intercessor."
See beginning of Book XI. of "Paradise Lost."

p. 52, l. 1, **popular government was the most frugal.**
Apparently based on a statement in Toland's "Life of Milton ; "
but does not fairly represent Milton's actual opinion.

l. 7, **without any national impoverishment.** Johnson's
views on economical matters, those which have to do with the
creation and distribution of wealth, are hopelessly superficial.
Johnson was a firm believer in the doctrine that any kind of
expenditure necessarily produced an increase of wealth. All
wealth spent in show tends to "impoverishment;" just as money
spent on musical performances or plays tends to "impoverishment." In other words it does not tend to reproduce itself as
material wealth. But this does not, of course, prove that such
an expenditure is useless in a wider sense, since the production
of material wealth is not the sole or principal aim of society.

l. 9, **Milton's republicanism.** Milton was a republican in
sympathy, but he did not believe much in Parliaments ; he was
quite willing to welcome a strong and irresponsible autocrat
like Cromwell, rather than submit to the rule of a Parliament
which gave way to the Presbyterian clergy. What made Milton
opposed to the monarchy was dislike, not so much of political,
as of theological control, his lofty contempt (not without a
tincture of Pharisaism) for the dissoluteness and frivolity of a
court, and the "perpetual bowings and cringings of an abject
people" which offended his strong sense of personal dignity. He
dwells so much on this last point in his "Ready Way of Esta-
blishing a Free Commonwealth" that Johnson may almost be
pardoned for speaking of his "envious hatred of greatness."

l. 22, **Turkish contempt for females.** By the Mohamme-
dans females are put on quite a different level from that of
men. They are not allowed to take part in public worship, and
will not be admitted to heaven—at any rate to the same heaven
as men. Practically women have scarcely any legal rights as
against husband or father.

Milton's own views about women are very low. Woman's
creation was a sort of afterthought. She exists only for the
sake of man; in her duty to her husband all her duties are included. The famous line, "He for God only, she for God in
him" (Paradise Lost," iv. 299) is not an isolated utterance, but
completely sums up the general teaching of Milton. Compare
"Paradise Lost," iv. 440, *seq.* ; iv. 686, *seq.* We cannot discount
these latter passages, which are from the mouth of Eve, by calling them dramatic. Milton was so individual, and so very un-
dramatic a writer, that we are bound to take them literally,
especially since they harmonize exactly with other passages

avowedly expressing the author's own opinion. The passages
in Books VIII. and X., which dwell on marriage, are sensual
and unideal. His works on divorce all point in the same direction. And in the "De Doctrinâ Christianâ" he defends poly-
gamy as lawful under the Gospel (Bohn, ii. 225-287). The truth
is that Milton from his constant study of the Old Testament
and his dislike of the ascetic system of the Church, was
almost Oriental in his opinions and feelings about women.

l. 28, his sister. See p. 2.

l. 31, Crown-office. The Crown office of the Court of Chancery. See p. 82.

l. 34, Sir Christopher. See pp. 1, 52, 82. He lived at Ipswich.
He was buried in the church of St. Nicholas, Ipswich, March 22,
1692. His daughters, Mary and Catherine, were living at
Holloway about the year 1734; one of them died, according to
Hawkins, at the age of ninety-two. "Their parentage was
known to few; and their names were corrupted into Melton"
(Hawkins' note).

p. 53, l. 1, left a daughter. "She died 26th July, 1769,
housekeeper to Dr. Secker" (Cunningham). Dr. Secker, Archbishop of Canterbury, died in 1768.

l. 4, though deformed. In his deposition in the matter
of Milton's will, Sir Christopher speaks of Anne as "lame and
helpless." Another witness says she could earn her living by
"the making of gold and silver lace which the deceased bred her
up to."

That little love subsisted between Milton and his third wife
on the one hand, and his daughters on the other, is certain.
He described them to his brother, when the latter was witness
of his will, as "undutiful and unkind to him, not expressing any
particulars, but in former times he [Christopher] hath heard him
complain that they were careless of him, being blind, and made
nothing of deserting him." They had in fact been "living apart
from their father four or five years last past." The poet had told
another witness that when he was about to be married to his
third wife, Mary, the second daughter had said to a servant that
"it was no news to hear of his wedding, but if she could hear of
his death, that was something, and that his children did combine together and cause his maid servant to cheat him in her
marketings," and had "made away some of his books," and
would have "sold the rest to the dunghill women."

l. 6, Deborah. She is described as remarkably like the portraits of Milton. "Mr. Addison was desirous to see her once,
and desired she would bring with her testimonials of being
Milton's daughter; but as soon as she came into the room he
told her she needed none, her face being much of the likeness of

the pictures he had seen of him" (Letter from George Vertue to Charles Christian, printed by Cunningham from the "Gentlemen's Magazine," 1776).

l. 9, the "**Metamorphoses.**" See above, p. 50, and p. 132.

l. 23, **unideal,** having no ideas connected with them.

l. 25, **Addison made a present.** He gave her a few guineas, and seems to have hoped to get her a government pension. Masson, vi. 752.

l. 26, **some establishment,** a small settled allowance.

l. 27, **Queen Caroline** (1682-1737). The wife of George II., a woman remarkable for her tact and ability, who made some pretensions to be a patron of literature, a part her husband was not qualified or, indeed, anxious to fulfil.

l. 30, **Fort St. George.** The old name of Madras, and still the official name. Caleb Clarke was apparently parish clerk there from 1717 to 1719, when he died.

l. 34, **Cock-lane.** This lane "near Shoreditch Church" is not the lane between Newgate Street and Smithfield, which was famous as the scene of operations of a sham ghost in 1762, when the place was visited by many thousands of persons, including Walpole and Dr. Johnson. See Boswell, Bohn, i. 323.

p. 54, l. 7, **a benefit.** A performance, the profits of which would be given to her. Johnson himself took an interest in the matter, he not only wrote a Prologue, spoken by Garrick, but addressed a letter to the "General Advertiser" to call attention to the performance. See Boswell's "Johnson," Bohn, i. 172-173.

l. 9, **Dr. Newton.** Thomas Newton (1704-1782), Bishop of Bristol, who had published an annotated edition of Milton's "Paradise Lost" and "Paradise Regained," and a famous "Dissertation on the Prophecies." He was a fellow-townsman of Dr. Johnson. See Boswell's "Johnson," Bohn, iv. 210.

l. 11, **Tonson.** The grandnephew of the original Jacob Tonson. See p. 42 and p. 124. The Tonsons had bought the copyright of Milton's poems and no doubt profited largely by the fact.

l. 16, **Islington.** Here she died in 1754.

l. 26, **nothing satisfied.** See the note at the end of the verses on "The Passion." Globe edit. p. 495.

l. 27, **nice,** particular.

l. 30, **by a man.** Perhaps Baretti, Johnson's Italian friend. See Boswell's "Johnson," i. 237, 286, *note.*

p. 55, l. 1, **sentiment.** See p. 119.

l. 3, **exercises on Gunpowder Treason.** The epigram "in Proditionem Bombardicam." Globe, pp. 597 *seq.* Aldine, ii. 348.

Milton wrote a long Latin poem on the Fifth of November,

which is considered one of the best of his early productions in
that tongue. Globe, pp. 601-606. Aldine, ii. 355.

l. 14, **preserved at Cambridge.** See p. 26, and p. 111.

l. 24, **neatness and elegance.** A very characteristic eighteenth
century utterance, which should be carefully noted.

l. 27, **in dandling the kid.** " Paradise Lost," iv. 343-4.

l. 30, "**Lycidas.**" What Johnson says about Lycidas is so
hopelessly inappreciative and wrong-headed that one is likely to
overlook even the good points in it, the protest against unreality
and affectation. See Introduction, p. xxv. Mark Pattison is
nearer the truth when he says, " In ' Lycidas ' we have reached
the high-water mark of English poesy and of Milton's own production. A period of a century and a half was to elapse before
poetry in England seemed, in Wordsworth's ' Ode on Immortality,' to be rising again towards the level of inspiration which
it had once attained in ' Lycidas.' "

l. 31, **numbers.** Verses, here metrical effects.

p. 56, l. 1, **Arethuse and Mincius.** " Lycidas," 85-6. Arethusa, the nymph of the fountain called after her, near Syra-
cuse, in Sicily. Mincius, the river Mincio, which flows by
Mantua. The two symbolize Theocritus, the Sicilian Greek,
and Virgil, who was born near Mantua, the two greatest pastoral
poets.

l. 2, **fauns with cloven heel.** " Lycidas," p. 85.

l. 3, **there is little grief.** Johnson overlooks the difference
between the directly felt feeling of the mourner and the same
feeling felt again by the poet and the artist. Wordsworth has
carefully marked this distinction in his preface to the " Lyrical
Ballads," now printed at the end of all good editions of his poems.
" Poetry is the spontaneous overflow of powerful feelings : it
takes its origin from emotions recollected in tranquility ; the
emotion is contemplated till, by a species of reaction, the tranquility gradually disappears, and an emotion kindred to that
which was before the subject of contemplation is gradually produced, and does itself actually exist in the mind." But, he
adds, the emotion is " qualified by various pleasures, so that, in
describing any pleasures whatsoever, which are voluntarily
described, the mind will, upon the whole, be in a state of enjoyment." The immediately felt emotion of the sufferer prompts
the expressions which are abrupt and harsh ; the idealized
emotion of the poet, what Wordsworth calls the " shadow " of
emotion, clothes itself in images and words of beauty.

l. 6, **disgusting.** See p. 138, top.

l. 9, **Cowley tells of Hervey.** " On the Death of Mr.
William Hervey." Cowley's " Miscellaneous Works " (1700),
p. 13.

l. 18, **to batten**, to feed. Properly an intransitive verb. Compare "Hamlet," III. iv. 67.

l. 24, **such as a college easily supplies.** Such as come naturally to a young man at college.

l. 29, **what is become.** We should say, what has become.

p. 57, l. 1, **polluted.** Johnson often uses strong words where milder would do, and uses them in a mild sense. Compare "disgusting," "malignity," "indecent" (for "indecorous"), etc.

l. 1, **irreverend.** This should be irreverent. But the form in the text occurs in all early editions of Johnson.

l. 9, **nice,** exact, particular.

l. 15, **Theobald has remarked.** Lewis Theobald (died 1744), a poor poet, but a distinguished Shakespearian scholar. He was the butt of Pope, and was made the hero of the "Dunciad" in its first form.

l. 35, **sullen.** Lonely, and wishing to remain alone.

p. 58, l. 2, **glowing embers.** "Il Penseroso," 79.

l. 2, **outwatches the North star.** "Outwatch the Bear" ("Il Penseroso," 87). "As the Bear never sets, this implies that the student sits up till daybreak, when all the stars disappear" (Keightley).

l. 7, **walks into the dark trackless woods.** Warton points out that Johnson is wrong. The pensive man waits till the sun shines before he takes his walk.

l. 8, **enthusiasm.** In the eighteenth century the word has nearly always a bad sense. It suggests want of mental control and balance. To call a man an enthusiast was to call him crazy. Thus Locke devotes to religious enthusiasm a whole chapter in his "Essay on Human Understanding" (bk. iv. ch. xix.), in which he speaks of it as "rising from the conceits of a warmed or overweening brain."

expects, awaits.

l. 11, **Mirth and Melancholy,** sc. as they are represented in Milton's two poems. They depict the gaiety and pensiveness of the cultivated student.

l. 15, **participation of.** We should say participation in.

l. 26, **delight in musick.** Cf. the beautiful lines, "L'Allegro," 135, seq., "Il Penseroso," 161, seq. Milton himself was a musician and the son of a musician. See pp. 1, 82, 131.

l. 28, **dismission,** dismissal. The word is now obsolete.

solemn sounds, sc., of Orpheus. The poets represent Orpheus as singing solemnly. The early fragments which were, of course wrongly, attributed to him were chiefly hymns.

l. 35, **colours of the diction,** the character of the language employed.

p. 59, l. 17, **period,** complete sentence.

l. 29, **its convenience**, *sc.*, as a feature in the plot, or plan, of the piece.

l. 34, **no precedents can support it.** This is an instance of Johnson's regard for common-sense criticism (Introduction, p. xxii.). To make one of the characters in a play address the audience can never, he says, be admissible; however great the authority of those writers who have done it.

p. 60, l. 1, **discourse of the Spirit**, the opening discourse addressed to the audience, vv. 1-92.

l. 14, **the song**, vv. 280 *seq.*

l. 19, **how fine it is,** vv. 476 *seq.*

l. 27, **of no use because it is false.** Johnson seems to mean that there was no need for the Spirit to tell an elaborate fiction to account for his presence and the assistance he can give them.

It is, perhaps, just possible that Johnson wrote : " of no use; *besides* it is false, and therefore," etc.

p. 61, l. 4, **figures are too bold,** the figures of speech—metaphor, metonymy, synecdoche, and so forth. Johnson, true to the leading ideal of his criticism, common-sense, finds much the same fault with Shakespeare : " The equality of words to things is very often neglected, and trivial sentiments and vulgar [ordinary] ideas disappoint the attention, to which they are recommended by sonorous epithets and swelling figures " (Preface to " Shakespeare ").

l. 10, **they are not bad.** When Hannah More " expressed a wonder that the poet who had written ' Paradise Lost,' should write such poor sonnets," Johnson said, " Milton, Madam, was a genius who could carve a Colossus from a rock, but could not carve heads upon cherry-stones." (Boswell, Bohn, iv. 228.) For a truer appreciation of Milton's sonnets, see Wordsworth's sonnet, " Scorn not the Sonnet " (1827).

l. 10, **the eighth and twenty-first.** These are the sonnets: " When the Assault was intended to the City," and the first addressed to Cyriack Skinner (Globe edit., pp. 546, 552 ; Aldine, i, 98, 106). So that the sonnets on the " Massacre in Piedmont " and on his Blindness are not " entitled to this slender commendation " of being " not bad."

l. 5, **a drama in the epic style,** a drama which presents the action rather in the fashion of a lofty narrative than by exhibiting the deeds of the actors themselves.

l. 14, **greater variety of termination,** and therefore fewer rhymes. The proper, or Italian, form of sonnet only allows two rhymes in the first eight lines.

l. 23, **first praise of genius,** the praise of being possessed of the highest genius.

l. 35, **by retrospection and anticipation.** An epic poem

should, according to the classical critics, contain a retrospective account of the events which occurred before the actions described in the first book (which usually plunges, as Horace advised, *in medias res*), and an anticipatory account of events which shall happen as a kind of sequel after the proper action of the poem is concluded. Thus, in the "Æneid," bks. ii. and iii. relate the story of the wanderings of the hero before his arrival at Carthage, with which event bk. i. opens ; the last part of bk. viii. foretells the future glories of Rome. In the "Paradise Lost," the latter part of bk. v. and all bk. vi. relate the events which lead up to the overwhelming of Satan and his angels, with which the epic begins ; and in bks. xi.-xii. we get a prophetic account of the future history of mankind.

morality, moral philosophy, ethics.

p. 62, l. 2, **physiology**, the knowledge of nature in general ; not that comparatively narrow science we now call physiology. Cf. p. 11 and p. 98.

l. 5, **realizing fiction**, putting imaginary things before us like realities.

Note that Johnson's account of the equipment of the poet leaves out of sight the need of emotion. Wordsworth puts this first. The poet, he says, is a man " endowed with more lively sensibility, more enthusiasm and tenderness, who has a greater knowledge of human nature, and a more comprehensive soul, than are supposed to be common among mankind ; a man pleased with his own passions and volitions, and who rejoices more than other men in the spirit of life that is in him " (Preface to the " Lyrical Ballads ").

l. 10, **Bossu**. René le Bossu (1631-1680), a French priest and critic, whose treatise on epic poetry (1675), was the standard work on the subject during the fifty years which followed its publication. See Hallam, " European Literature," iv. 305.

On Bossu and his theory, " that an epic writer first of all pitches upon a certain moral as the groundwork and foundation of his poem," see Addison, in the " Spectator," No. 369.

l. 17, **vindicate the ways of God to man**. " Paradise Lost," i. 26. Milton, however, said, " justify the ways of God to men."

p. 63, l. 7, **his agents**, his actors, those who take part in the action of the poem.

l. 15, **of which the least could wield**. " Paradise Lost," vi. 221-223. Johnson's quotations are often, like this, verbally inexact.

l. 27, **which admit of examination**. God the Father and the Son appear as characters ; to examine these would, Johnson suggests, be irreverent.

l. 33. Abdiel.

" The seraph Abdiel faithful found,
Among the faithless, faithful only he."

He withstood Satan and the rebellious angels.   See Bk. v.
803, *seq.*, and Bk. vi. 1-43.

p. 64, l. 2, **as Addison observes.**   "His sentiments are every
way answerable to his character, and suitable to a created
being of the most exalted and most depraved nature " ("Spectator," No. 303).

Addison's famous essays on "Paradise Lost" occupy Nos.
267, 273, 279, 285, 291, 297, 303, 309, 315, 321, 327, 333, 339,
345, 351, 357, 363, 369 of the "Spectator."   They appeared
every Saturday for eighteen weeks, the Saturday "Spectator"
having been usually set apart for moral or religious topics.

l. 4, **by Clarke.**   "Author of the 'Essay on Study'" (Johnson's note).   This was John Clarke, Master of the Grammar
School at Hull.   He published his "Essay on Study," a practical treatise on the method of study and the formation of a
library, in 1731.   Clarke translated and edited several of the
Latin classics.   Some of his educational works were very
popular.

l. 21, **Moloch.**   Milton describes him as

" the strongest and the fiercest spirit
That fought in Heaven, now fiercer by despair."
"Paradise Lost," ii. 44-5.

See also i. 392-93.   Compare "Spectator," No. 309.

p. 65, l. 3, **vulgar,** ordinary.

l. 4, **immerge,** immerse.   This form is almost obsolete,
though more correct.

l. 14, **remarked by Addison.**   "Milton's subject was still
greater than either of the former [those of the 'Iliad' and the
' Æneid ']; it does not determine the fate of single persons or
nations, but of a whole species " ("Spectator," No. 267).   "The
principal actors in this poem are not only our progenitors, but
our representatives.   We have an actual interest in everything
they do, and no less than our utmost happiness is concerned
and lies at stake in all their behaviour " (No. 278).

l. 20, **the machinery.** " The machinery, madam, is a term in-
vented by the critics to signify that part which the deities, angels,
or demons are made to act in a poem " (Pope, Dedication to the
" Rape of the Lock ").   " No heroic poem," says Dryden, " can
be writ on the Epicurean principles," that is, on the assumption
that the Gods do not care for the affairs of mankind.

Θεὸς ἀπὸ μηχανῆς, the god out of the machine.   The machine
in question was a stage contrivance for the appearance and dis-

appearance of the gods. The "deus ex machina" was brought
on to solve the difficulties of a situation. Horace requires that
he shall only be brought on when the difficulty is worthy of
such interference ("Ars Poetica," 191-192). This is "the rule"
referred to in l. 24.

l. 27, **episodes,** narratives introduced into the main narrative
for the purpose of variety. Such episodes should be naturally
connected with the principal action. Compare note to p. 61,
l. 32.

l. 84, **what Aristotle requires.** "Poetics," Part II.,
chap. iv.

p. 66, l. 19, **petulantly and indecently,** without sufficient
reason or sufficient seriousness.

l. 19, **the heroism of Adam,** that Adam is the hero. Dryden, in
his "Discourse of Epic Poetry," prefixed to the translation of
the "Æneid," had complained that the devil was Milton's hero,
not Adam. On which Addison remarks that "he that looks for
a hero in it, searches for that which Milton never intended;
but if he will needs fix the name of an hero upon any person in
it, 'tis certainly the Messiah who is the hero" ("Spectator,"
No. 297).

l. 23, **Cato is the hero of Lucan.** The "Pharsalia" of the
Roman poet, Marcus Annæus Lucanus (89 A.D.-65 A.D.), relates
the struggle between Cæsar and Pompey.

l. 24, **Quintilian.** Marcus Fabius Quintilianus (c. 40 A.D.,
c. 100 A.D.), a great Roman rhetorician and critic. His "De In-
stitutione Oratoria" is a complete system of rhetoric in twelve
books, and had the highest authority, not only among classical,
but also modern scholars. Quintilian considers that Lucan is
not to be imitated by poets so much as by orators (x., i. 90;
ed. Halm, p. 220).

l. 81, **sentiments.** See p. 119.

p. 67, l. 1, **no human manners.** By "manners" Aristotle
and the critics mean, "whatever marks the character of the persons" (Aristotle, "Poetics," II., ii.). Adam and Eve before
the Fall were in a position so different from that of all mankind
since, that their speech and behaviour must have been quite
different.

l. 5, **Abdiel maintained.** See p. 63 and p. 140.

l. 6, **accommodated,** applied to.

l. 7. **Raphael's reproof.** "Paradise Lost," viii. 159, *seq.*

l. 9, **opposed to,** put in rivalry to, without fear of being found
inferior.

l. 15, **curiosity.** In a good sense; while in l. 8 it is, of
course, used in a bad.

l. 16, **sublimate,** to refine and purify. In chemistry, to sub-

limate a solid substance is to raise it to a state of vapour, and
then let it condense in a cool vessel into a solid again; sublima-
tion is thus a corresponding process to the distillation of liquids.
One result of it is to secure the substance in a purer form.

l. 21, **extensive**, of great magnitude. Great size is one of the
conditions which produce the feeling of sublimity. Milton
pictures for us enormous beings of enormous power inhabiting
enormous places. Compare bottom of p. 68.

p. 68, l. 3, **rather than the fancy.** By fancy Dr. Johnson
means the productive imagination, the power of picturing things
not actually experienced.

l. 19, **as Dryden expresses it.** "Essay of Dramatic Poesy,"
p. 53 (Univ. Corr. Coll. edit.). " He [Shakespeare] was naturally
learned : he needed not the spectacles of books to read Nature ;
he looked inwards and found her there."

l. 22, **the vale of Enna.**

> " Not that fair field
> Of Enna, where Proserpine gathering flowers,
> Herself a fairer flower, by gloomy Dis
> Was gathered, which cost Ceres all that pain
> To seek her through the world."
> 　　　　　　　" Paradise Lost," iv. 268, *seq.*

Milton follows the classical simile with several others. Enna
was in Sicily; one of the chief temples of Demeter, or Ceres,
stood there.

l. 24, **like Argo.**

> " Harder beset
> And more endangered than when Argo passed
> Through Bosporus betwixt the justling rocks ;
> Or when Ulysses on the larboard shunned
> Charybdis, and by the other whirlpool steered."
> 　　　　　　　" Paradise Lost," ii. 1016, *seq.*

The Cyanean rocks, otherwise called the Symplegades (or clashing rocks) were two rocky islets at the Euxine mouth of the
Bosphorus. They were said to clash together on all vessels,
until Jason passed them safely in the Argo; after which they
became stationary.

l. 26, **Charybdis.** The poets differ in their account of Scylla
and Charybdis. Homer makes them to be both rocks ; though
Charybdis, who dwelt on one, swallows down the water of the
sea, thrice every day, and thrice throws it back. Other poets
make one a rock and one a whirlpool ; while others still represent them as two whirlpools.

l. 28, **with notice of their vanity**, with notice that they were (unlike the Scriptural similes) fictitious.

p. 69, l. 1, **the shield of Satan.** "Paradise Lost," i. 284, *seq.*

"The broad circumference
Hung on his shoulders like the moon, whose orb
Through optic glass the Tuscan artist views
At evening, from the top of Fesolé
Or in Valdarno, to descry new lands,
Rivers, or mountains, on her spotty globe."

On the similes of Milton see the "Spectator," No. 303.

l. 10, **amiable**, lovable.

l. 17, **Ariosto's pravity.** "Pravity" here means vice, depravity.

Ariosto (1475-1533), the Italian poet, whose great epic the "Orlando Furioso," in forty cantos, was published in 1516, and in an enlarged form in 1532. It became one of the most popular poems in Europe; above sixty editions were published in the sixteenth century. Its subject is the wars of Charlemain and his paladins with the Saracens. See Hallam, "Literature of Europe," i. 309, *seq.*

l. 18, "**Deliverance of Jerusalem.**" The subject of Tasso's great epic, "La Gerusalemme Liberata," completed 1575 and published 1581. Torquato Tasso (1544-1595), who also wrote a pastoral play, "Aminta," and other works, is considered among the Italian poets second only to Dante. See Hallam, "Literature of Europe," ii. 198, *seq.*

p. 70, l. 8, **the port of mean suitors.** "Paradise Lost," xi. 8, 9.

"Yet their port
Not of mean suitors."

l. 20, **sometimes argumentative**, sometimes exhibited in the arguments held by the different persons in the poem.

l. 24, **to discover**, to exhibit, set forth.

l. 32, **Bentley.** Richard Bentley (1662-1742), the greatest classical scholar England has produced. He was Master of Trinity College, Cambridge, from 1700 till his death. His chief works are his "Dissertation on the Epistles of Philasis," his editions of Horace and Terence, and his lamentable edition of Milton (1732), which suggests doubts as to the validity of the methods of classical textual criticism.

l. 34, **sometimes made them**, sometimes only imagined they were there.

l. 35, **obtrusions**, intrusions, the thrusting of himself forward.

p. 71, l. 5, **human manners.** See p. 67, l. 1, and note, p. 142.

l. 18, **surely,** certainly, inevitably.

l. 29, **their association,** their being brought into one company, before their attention.

p. 72, l. 1, **too ponderous for the wings of wit,** too mighty for mere intelligence to deal with.

l. 7, **pregnancy,** inventive force.

l. 8, **radical positions,** statements lying at the root, and forming a basis for the poem.

l. 12, **licentiousness,** licence, improper freedom.

l. 23, **deficience.** Obsolete; we say " deficiency."

p. 73, l. 9, **burning marle.** " Paradise Lost," i. 295, *seq.*

> " His spear . . .
> He walked with, to support uneasy steps
> Over the burning marle."

Marl is a mixture of clay and chalk; but the word is perhaps here used to mean simply sticky soil, unpleasant to walk on.

l. 12, **when he animates the toad.** " Paradise Lost," iv. 800.

l. 14, **he starts up in his own steps.** " Paradise Lost," iv. 819.

l. 16, **a spear and a shield.** " Paradise Lost," iv. 989-990.

> " Nor wanted in his grasp
> What seemed both spear and shield."

l. 19, **Pandæmonium,** the palace of the demons in hell.

l. 20, **though without number.** " Paradise Lost," i. 789.

l. 22, **crushed in upon their substance.** *Ib.,* vi. 656, *seq.*

l. 25, **the sooner for their arms.** *Ib.,* vi. 595, *seq.* :

> " Unarmed they might
> Have easily, as spirits, evaded swift
> By quick contraction or remove."

l. 31, **when he rides on a sunbeam.** *Ib.,* iv. 589-591.

l. 32, **when he is afraid.** *Ib.,* ix. 481-485.

p. 74, l. 1, **in which it is related.** Bk. vi.

l. 16, **" Prometheus " of Æschylus.** Æschylus (525-456, B.C.), first of the great Athenian tragic poets, is said to have written seventy tragedies. The " Prometheus Vinctus," which is one of the seven which have come down to us, was produced between 470 and 458 B.C.

l. 17, **" Alcestis " of Euripides.** On Euripides, see p. 132. The " Alcestis " was produced in 438, B.C.

l. 18, **as active persons in the drama.** The old " Moralities '' were acted allegories, in which nearly all the characters were

Virtues and Vices. In early plays, Bishop Bale's "King John" for instance, allegorical characters were frequently introduced side by side with actual persons. See Addison in the "Spectator," No. 273.

l. 20, **allegory of Sin and Death.** See "Paradise Lost," ii. 648-814. Compare Addison, "Spectator," No. 309.

l. 84, **aggravated soil.** So all editions of Johnson's " Lives"; but Milton wrote " aggregated ":

> " The aggregated soil
> Death with his mace petrific, cold and dry,
> As with a trident smote, and fixed as firm
> As Delos floating once ; the rest his look
> Bound with Gorgonian rigour not to move,
> And with asphaltic slime."
> 　　　　　　　　　　"Paradise Lost," x. 293-298.

asphaltus, bitumen.

l. 85, **ideal,** imaginary, unreal.

p. 75, l. 5, **with great expectation,** a great deal of care and elaboration is given to the account, so that the reader is led to expect that something important is about to be described. See " Paradise Lost," iv. 877-1015.

l. 9, **rife in heaven.** "Paradise Lost," i. 650.

l. 12, **something of anticipation.** Adam and Eve are sometimes drawn as though they had already the knowledge which would come from experience.

l. 13, **discovered,** disclosed.

discourse of dreams. "Paradise Lost," v. 95, *seq.*

l. 15, **answer to the angel's reproof.** "Paradise Lost," viii. 179, *seq.*

l. 20, **timorous deer.** According to Prendergast's "Concordance," no mention is made of deer in " Paradise Lost." Johnson was probably thinking of the "timorous flock " in vi. 857. Sin had not yet blighted the earth with death and fear, which, as the Bible says, came in with the Fall of Man. Cf. x. 706, *seq.,* xi. 182, *seq.*

l. 22, **Dryden remarks.** " Milton's ' Paradise Lost' is admirable; but am I therefore bound to maintain that there are no flats among his elevations, when it is evident he creeps along sometimes for a hundred lines together ? " (Preface to " Tonson's Second Miscellany," 1685). And again, " It is true he runs into a flat of thought, sometimes for a hundred lines together, but it is when he is got into a tract of scripture " (" Discourse on Satire," 1692 ; Cassell's Nat. Lib. edit., p. 22).

l. 30, **expatiated,** wandered freely. The Lat., *expatiari,* to wander, is for *ex-spatiari,* from *ex* and *spatium.*

p. 76, l. 1, **Ariosto's levity.** On Ariosto, see note to p. 69, l. 17. " It has been sometimes hinted as an objection to Ariosto, that he is not sufficiently in earnest, and leaves a little suspicion of laughing at his subject. I do not perceive that he does this in a greater degree than good sense and taste permit. . . . It is the light carelessness of his manner which constitutes a great part of its charm" (Hallam, "Literature of Europe," i. 810). Addison says, "Such allegories [as the Limbo of Vanity] rather savour of the spirit of Spenser and Ariosto, than of Homer and Virgil" ("Spectator," No. 297).

l. 2, **"Paradise of Fools."** "Paradise Lost," iii. 440-497. There is an allusion to Ariosto ("Orlando Furioso," xxxiv. 70) in line 459 ; and Milton had already alluded to Ariosto's treatment of the subject, in his pamphlet "Of Reformation in England" ("Prose Works," Bohn, ii. 383-884). The notion that somewhere beyond the grave there was a resting-place for fools and idiots and the trifles which amuse them, is to be found in many early poets, and is based on the scholastic doctrine of a *limbus fatuorum.*

l. 4, **play on words.** For instances and criticism, see Addison, "Spectator," No. 279 (end), 297. Amongst Addison's instances are :

" Begirt th' Almighty throne,
Beseeching or besieging."

"This tempted our attempt."

"At one slight bound high overleapt all bound."

l. 5, **Bentley endeavours to defend.** Bentley on the contrary speaks of them as " deservedly censured," but attributes some of them to the imaginary editor, whom he made responsible for all he disapproved. See Bentley's note to i. 642.

l. 7, **terms of art,** technical terms. Here also Johnson follows Addison, "Spectator," No. 297: "The last fault," he says, "I shall take notice of in Milton's style is the frequent use of what the learned call technical terms, or terms of art."

l. 13, **nice,** delicate, refined.

l. 30, **a chorus.** The chorus was an essential feature of the Greek drama; it explains the plot, moralizes on it, and sometimes actually takes part in the action. "The chorus," says Aristotle, "Poetics," II. xxi., "should be considered as one of the persons in the drama; should be a part of the whole, and a sharer in the action."

p. 77, l. 1, **particular beauties.** Beauties of detail as opposed to those of general form.

l. 6, **in the gross**, as a whole.

l. 18, **peculiarity of Diction**. On this, see Addison, "Spectator," No. 285 and No. 297. Addison, on the whole, defends Milton's use of foreign words and idioms. Compare Richardson on "Paradise Lost," p. cxlii.: "Milton's language is English, but 'tis Milton's English: 'tis Latin, 'tis Greek English; not only the words, the phraseology, the transpositions, but the ancient idiom, is seen in all he wrote."

l. 21, **says Addison**. "Our language sunk under him, and was unequal to that greatness of soul which furnished him with such glorious conceptions " ("Spectator," No. 297).

Richardson had said practically the same thing (p. cxlii.).

l. 24, **English words with a foreign idiom**. Compare the following from a letter of John Keats: "The 'Paradise Lost,' so fine in itself, is a corruption of our language—a beautiful and grand curiosity—a Northern dialect accommodating itself to Greek and Latin inversions and intonations."

l. 84, **the Tuscan poets**. The poets of Italy, Dante, Ariosto, Tasso, etc.

disposition, arrangement.

p. 78, l. 2, **what Jonson says of Spenser**. "Spenser, in affecting the ancients, wrote no language; yet would I have him read for his matter as Virgil read Ennius " (Ben Jonson, "Discoveries," Cassell's National Library edition, pp. 106-107; compare p. 118).

l. 4, **what Butler calls**. Samuel Butler, "Hudibras," Part I., canto i.:

> " But, when he pleas'd to shew't, his speech
> In loftiness of sound was rich;
> A Babylonish dialect,
> Which learned pedants much affect;
> It was a party-colour'd dress
> Of patch'd and piebald languages:
> 'Twas English cut on Greek and Latin
> Like fustian heretofore on satin."

Babylon and Babel appear to be in origin the same word. Compare Genesis xi.

Mrs. Napier quotes Hallam's remark, that out of Milton's love of verbal melody arose "one of his trifling faults, the excessive passion he displays for stringing together sonorous names, sometimes so obscure that the reader associates nothing with them " (Hallam, "Literature of Europe," iv. 241).

l. 13, **his versification**. On versification, compare Johnson, "Rambler," Nos. 86, 88, 90, 94. A modern authority on Milton's verse is Mr. Robert Bridges.

l. 14, he says. See Milton's introductory note to "Paradise Lost" on "The Verse" (Globe edit., p. 41; Aldine i. 148).

l. 17, Earl of Surrey. Henry Howard, Earl of Surrey (c. 1517-1547), translated *two* books of Virgil, not one, as Johnson supposed. His blank verse translation of bks. ii. and iv. of the " Æneid " appeared in 1557, or earlier.

l. 18, a few short poems. For instance, two poems of about one hundred lines each, by Grimald, in "Tottel's Miscellany" (1557). Johnson probably overlooked Gascoigne's "Steel Glass" (1576), a poem of over eleven hundred lines.

l. 20, Written by Raleigh himself. "'De Guiana Carmen Epicum. Authore G. C.' Printed in Hakluyt, vol. iii. Oldys attributes it to George Chapman. Sufficient attention has not been paid to this early and thoughtful specimen of blank verse " (Cunningham).

l. 24, Trisino's "Italia Liberata." Giovanni Trissino (1478-1550), published his "Italia Liberata" in 1548. "No one has ever pretended to rescue from the charge of dulness and insipidity the epic poem of the father of blank verse, Trissino, on the liberation of Italy from the Goths by Belisarius. It is, of all long poems that are remembered at all, the most unfortunate in its reputation" (Hallam, "Literature of Europe," i. 422).

l. 27, he says. Note on "The Verse." "Rime being no necessary adjunct, or true ornament of poem or good verse, in longer works especially, but the invention of a barbarous age, to set off wretched matter and lame metre."

l. 28, as a mental operation, that is, as not yet expressed in words.

p. 79, l. 11, an ingenious critic. This, as Boswell relates, was "Mr. Lock, of Norbury Park, in Surrey, whose knowledge and taste in the fine arts is universally celebrated" ("Life of Johnson," Bohn, iv. 8).

Another "ingenious critic," Cowper the poet, asks, "Was there ever anything so delightful as the music of 'Paradise Lost'? It is like that of a fine organ; has the fullest and deepest notes of majesty, with all the softness and elegance of the Dorian flute. Variety without end, and never equalled, unless perhaps by Virgil" (Cowper to Unwin, October 31st, 1779).

Dryden bluntly affirms that "Milton's own particular reason" (for not using rhyme) "is plainly this—that rhyme was not his talent; he had neither the ease of doing it, nor the graces of it, which is manifest in his 'Juvenilia,' or verses written in his youth, where the rhyme is always constrained and forced, and comes hardly from him, at an age when the soul is most pliant, and the passion of love makes almost every man a rhymer,

though not a poet " ("Discourse of Satire," Cassell's National
Library, pp. 22-28).

l. 16, **lapidary style,** the style in which monumental inscriptions are written. See p. 8 and p. 90.

l. 19, **whom Milton alleges.** "Not without cause, therefore,
since both Italian and Spanish poets of prime note have rejected
rime both in longer and shorter works" (Note on "The Verse ").

l. 81, **that vigour and amplitude of mind,** to that vigorous
and mighty mind, viz., Homer. Compare Introduction, p. xxiii.
above.

p. 80, l. 9, **no exchange of praise,** no interchange of compli-
ments with other authors.

INDEX.

Academies, Italian, 7, 90.
Act of Oblivion, 31, 114, 115.
"Adams," The, of Andreini, 35, 119.
"Adam Unparadised," 28.
Addison, 53, 64, 65, 77, 136, 141, 148.
Æschylus, 74, 145.
Agar, 52.
"Alabaster," 3, 84.
Aldersgate-Street, 10, 92.
Allegory, 14.
Ames, Dr., 94.
Anglesey, Earl of, 45, 126.
"Arcadia," 19, 87, 104.
Arethusa, 137.
Ariosto, 69, 144.
Aristotle, 65.
Arminianism, 133.
Articles, Subscription to the Thirty-nine, 5.
Artillery Walk, 35, 118.
Ascham, 3, 84.
Atterbury, 48, 129.
Aubrey, 81, 129, 130, *et passim*.
Aylmer, 42, 124.

Barberini, Cardinal, 8, 91.
Barbican, 17.
Bartholomew Close, 31, 114.
Benson, 48, 129.

Bentley, 70, 76, 144, 147.
Betterton, 32, 116.
Birch, Dr., 19, 105.
Blackborough, Mr., 16.
Blank verse, 78.
Bossu, 62.
Bramhall, Archbishop, 23, 109.
Bucer, Martin, 15.
Bunhill Fields, 41.
Burnet, 32.
Butler, 78.

"Cabinet Council," 30, 112.
Calvin, 133.
Cambridge Latin Dictionary, 25, 110.
Caroline, Queen, 53, 136.
Caston, 1, 82.
Chalfont, 41, 123.
Chapman, 149.
Charybdis, 143.
Chorus in classical plays, 76, 147.
Christina, Queen of Sweden, 7, 21, 90, 107.
Clarges, Sir Thomas, 32, 115.
Clark, Abraham, 53.
Clark, Caleb, 53.
Clark, Deborah, 53.
Clarke, John, 64, 141.
Cock Lane, 53, 136.

Corporal punishment at the Universities, 3, 85.
Cowley, 2, 11, 50, 56, 83, 93.
Cowper, 149.
Cradock, 50, 132.
Cromwell, 22, 23, 24.
Crown-office, 2, 82.
Cyanean rocks, 143.

Dalrymple, Sir John, 32, 115.
Dati, Carlo, 8.
Davenant, 32, 116.
Davis, Dr., 16.
"Defensio Regia," 20, 106.
Diction, 77.
Diodati, Charles, 3, 9, 85.
Diodati, John, 9.
Dryden, 50, 66, 68, 75, 143, 146, 149.
Du Moulin, Peter, 23, 109.

Elwood, 34, 41, 45, 46, 117, *seq.*, 127, *et passim.*
Epic poetry, 61, *seq.*
Episodes, 65, 142.
Euripides, 51, 53, 132, 145.

Fenton, 1, 26, 81, 111.
Florence, 7.
Fort St. George, 53, 136.
Francini, 8, 90.

Galileo, 9, 91.
Geneva, 9.
Geoffrey of Monmouth, 45, 126.
Gill, 2, 83.
Goodman, Dr., 121.
Goodwin, Dr., 31, 114.
Gregory, Dr., 48, 129.
Griffith, Dr., 30, 113.
Grotius, 7, 90, 119.
Groto, 85.

Haddon, 13, 84.
Hall, Bishop, 12, 94.
Hall, Robert, 96, *seq.*
Hampton, 3, 84.
Harefield, 7, 89.
Harrington, 30, 113.
Hartlib, 4, 86, 118.
Hervey, William, 56, 137.
Hobbes, 20, 106.
Holborn, 18.
Holstenius, 8, 90.
Homer, 6, *seq.*, 79, *seq.*
Horton, 6, 88.
Howel, 16, 92, 100.

"Icon Basilike," 19, 104.
Italian poetry, 6.

Jeffrey, Paul, 82.
Jesuits, 9.
Jewin Street, 33, 116.
Jonson, 78.
Juvenal, 21, 107.
Juxon, Archbishop, 19, 105.

Keats, 148.
Ker, 20, 107.
King, Edward, 6.

Lapidary style, 8, 79, 90.
Lawes, Henry, 88.
Leigh, Lady Margaret, 15, 98.
L'Estrange, 30, 114.
Licensing of books, 123, 126.
Lucan, 66, 142.
Ludlow, 89.

Machinery, 65.
Manso, Marquis of Villa, 8, 9, 26, 91.
Marvell, 32, 115.
Mask, Masque, 29, 59, 88.

· Milton, Anne (Milton's sister), 2.
Milton, Deborah, 53, 135.
Milton, John, the father of the
    poet, 1, 82.
Milton, John, the poet.
    Appearance, 36, 48.
    Birth, 2.
    Blindness, 22, 108.
    Controversial manner, 13, 87,
      95, *seq.*
    Daughters, 44, 108, 134.
    Death, 47, 128.
    Diction, 77, 147.
    Dwellings, 6, 18, 31, 114, 116,
      118, 123.
    Education, his, 2-6 ; his plan
      of education, 10, 11.
    Fame, 42, 125.
    Family, 44, 52, *seq.*, 134.
    Habits, 36, *seq.*, 48, *seq.*
    Latin secretary, 19, 49.
    Learning, 50.
    Marriages, 15, 22, 33, 98,
      108.
    Money affairs, 49, *seq.*, 131,
      seq.
    Monument, 47, *seq.*, 128, *seq.*
    Political opinions, 51, *seq.*,
      134.
·   Theological opinions, 50, *seq.*,
      100, 135.
    Will, 33, 116, *seq.*
  Works :
    " Accidence   commenced
      Grammar," 34.
    " Animadversions upon the
      Remonstrant's Defence,"
      96, 97.
    " Apology against ' A Modest
      Confutation,' " 96.
    " Arcades," 7, 89.
    " Areopagitica," 17.

Milton, John—*continued.*
    " Artis Logicæ Institutio,"
      46.
    " Colasterion," 100.
    " Comus," 6, 59, *seq.*
    "Considerations touching the
      likeliest Means of Re-
      moving Hirelings," 4, 30,
      86.
    " De Doctrina Christiana,"
      128.
    " Doctrine and Discipline of
      Divorce," 15, 91.
    " Eikonoklastes," 19, 105.
    " Epistolarum Familiarum
      liber," 47, 128.
    " Epitaphium Damonis," 9.
    " History of Britain," 45,
      126.
    "Judgment of Martin Bucer,"
      15, 98.
    " L'Allegro and Il Pense-
      roso," 17, 57, *seq.*
    Latin Poems, 9, 54.
    " Lycidas," 6, 55, 89, 137.
    " Of Education," 86.
    " Of Prelatical Episcopacy,"
      13.
    " Of Reformation in Eng-
      land," 12.
    " Paradise Lost," 25, 35, 40-
      44, 61, *seq.*, 125.
    " Paradise Regained," 45, 46,
      61, *seq.*
    " Poems both English and
      Latin," 17.
    " Prolusiones Academicæ,"
      128.
    " Pro Populo Anglicano De-
      fensio," 20.
    " Pro Populo Anglicano De-
      fensio Secunda," 23.

Milton, John—*continued.*
"Pro Se Defensio contra Morum," 24.
"Ready and Easy Way to Establish a Free Commonwealth," 30.
"Reason of Church Government," 13, 96.
"Remarks on the Articles of Peace," 18.
"Samson Agonistes," 45.
Sonnets, 22, 61, 109.
"Tetrachordon,", 15, 99.
"Tenure of Kings and Magistrates," 103.
"Treatise of Civil Power," 30.
"Treatise of True Religion," 46, 128.
Milton, Mary. *See* Powell, Mary.
Milton, Sir Christopher, 1, 2, 52, 82, 135.
Mincius, 137.
Minshull, Elizabeth, 33, 116.
Morrice, 32, 115.
Morus, 24, 109.
Mysteries, 26, 111, 112.

Nantwich, 49.
Newton, Dr., 54, 136.

"Obstructors of Justice," 31.
Ovid, 50, 53, 89, 110, 132.

Paget, Dr., 33.
Paradise of fools, 76, 147.
Pastoral poetry, 56.
Pepys, 113.
Philips, Edward, 2, 12, 15, 16, 17, 25, 26, 33, 36, 44, 82, 92, 98, *et passim.*

Philips, John, 2, 23.
Philips, John (author of "Cyder"), 48, 129.
Play on words, 76, 147.
Plays at the Universities, 87.
Politian, 2, 83.
Powell, Mary, Milton's first wife, 15, 16.
Powell, Mr., 15, 16, 98, 101.
Press, freedom of the, 17.

Quintilian, 66.

Raleigh, 30, 78, 149.
Ramus, 46, 127.
Richardson, 32, 36, 37, 39, 48, 115, 119, *et passim.*
Rome, 8.
"Roxana," 3, 84.
Russel, 10.
Rustication, 3.

Salmacis, 20, 106.
Salmasius, 19, 20, 21, 22, 105.
Salsilli, 8, 91.
School, course of study in, 11.
Scudamore, Lord, 7, 90, 108.
Selvaggi, 8, 91.
Sentiments, 35, 69, 119.
Sidney, Sir Philip, 19, 87.
Sienna, 8.
Simmons, 41, 124.
Smectymnuus, 12, 95.
Socrates, 12, 93.
Spanheim, 9, 92.
Spenser, 50, 78.
Sprat, 48, 129.
St. Bride's Churchyard, 10, 92.
St. Giles, Cripplegate, 47.
St. Martin's-le-Grand, 16.
Surrey, Earl of, 78, 148.

Tasso, 8, 69, 144.
Theobald, 57, 138.
Toland, 30, 37, 113.
Tomkyns, 123, 127.
Tonson, 42, 54, 124, 136.
Tragedies, Classical, 76.
"Tractatulus de Carmine dramatico," 94.
Trisino, 78, 149.

Usher, Archbishop, 13, 95.

Venice, 9.

Versification, 78.
Voltaire, 35.

Waller, Sir William, 18.
Westminster Assembly, 15, 16, 99.
Wood, Anthony, 16, 36, 99.
Woodcock, Catherine, 22.
Wollebius, 94.
Wotton, Sir Henry, 7, 89.

Young, Thomas, 2, 83.

CHISWICK PRESS:—CHARLES WHITTINGHAM AND CO.
TOOKS COURT, CHANCERY LANE, LONDON.

CPSIA information can be obtained
at www.ICGtesting.com
Printed in the USA
BVOW04*1005250517

485105BV00013B/10/P